7-29-74

# The Buffet Cookbook

# The Buffet Cookbook

## HELEN SCHRADER

ARLINGTON HOUSE·PUBLISHERS

NEW ROCHELLE, N. Y.

1817207

To my family and friends
who encouraged me,
and then suffered for it.

# CONTENTS

# Buffet Entertaining

The word buffet is derived from the French and originally meant cupboard or sideboard. Now it is used to describe an informal meal where the guests serve themselves from a table, sideboard, shelves, or countertop. The buffet table may be placed either against a wall, so that the guests may have more room to eat at small tables, or else centered in the room so that the guests have more freedom to circulate around the table.

The appointments the hostess chooses for the table set the mood of the meal. Obviously, a table set with fine linens and china, silver serving pieces, and candelabra would be more formal than a table set with homespun, pottery and brass or copper. The centerpiece, whether an ornament or a flower arrangement, should also help set the mood.

Buffet meals allow the hostess to spend more time with the guests, but this is only accomplished if she has spent previous time planning, preparing and arranging all the necessary components. A buffet meal should be not only beautiful to look at, but also well balanced in flavors, calories, colors, and textures.

An additional advantage of buffet dining is that it allows the hostess more flexibility with regard to the number of guests and choice of dining area. Because there are no formal seating arrangements, this helps the guests feel more relaxed and contributes to the success of the party. They also have a choice as to the quantity and type of foods they choose to eat.

The plates, napkins, silver and serving dishes should be arranged in the order in which they will be needed. If your serving space is limited there are attractive tiered serving dishes which allow you to use space vertically. If you have your buffet table in one room and small tables scattered throughout other rooms, the napkins and silver should be preset on these small tables, rather than placed on the large buffet table.

Most of the recipes in this book can be prepared ahead, either completely and reheated, or partially assembled and finished just before serving. Casseroles and chafing dishes are especially easy to prepare in advance, and are also attractive on the buffet. Avoid foods that are hard to manage unless there are tables for all your guests.

Many of the foods included in the appetizer section can also be served with cocktails before dinner.

The recipes in this book are for 6, 8, 10, or 12 portions. They can be increased to serve more people, but it is much better to have two or three serving dishes of the same item, rather than one extra-large dish. In this way, the buffet always looks fuller, and the food fresher, to those who serve themselves later. It also allows the hostess to keep the reserved serving dishes either hot or cold, as the case may be.

Many of the recipes in the book are for what are commonly called "finger foods". These are not only easy for the guests to manage, but they also cut down on the required number of dishes and the after buffet clean up.

Coffee and dessert may be set on a separate smaller table or tea cart, or served after the main buffet table has been cleared.

All of the recipes in this book are not just limited to buffet entertaining, but can also be used for family and more formal sit-down dinners.

HELEN M. SCHRADER

## TERMS USED IN THIS BOOK

| | |
|---|---|
| tsp | teaspoon |
| T | tablespoon |
| C | cup |
| oz | ounce |
| lb | pound |
| pt | pint |
| qt | quart |
| pkg | package |

season to taste  The quantity of salt and pepper or paprika required varies due to natural differences in the foods used. The personal preferences and requirements of the cook may also call for adjustment in the quantity of seasonings required.

can size  I have used the common can size found in my locality in the recipes in this book. Most of the recipes can be made using a slight variation in size as packed by various manufacturers, ie: a 12-oz can can be substituted for a 10-1/2-oz can, and a 5-1/2-oz can can be substituted for a 6-oz can.

# Chapter 1

# APPETIZERS AND SNACKS

## BAKED CLAMS ITALIANO

1 can (10-1/2 oz) minced clams
2 T olive oil
1 T grated onion
1 T minced parsley
1/8 tsp oregano
1/4 C *plus* 2 T bread crumbs
1 tsp garlic salt
2 T grated Parmesan cheese

Drain clams and reserve 3 T broth. Heat olive oil in small frying pan. Sauté onion, parsley, oregano and 1/4 cup bread crumbs for 2 minutes, or until onion is golden. Remove from heat and mix with clams, 3 T broth, and garlic salt. Spoon into a dozen clam or aluminum shells. Sprinkle lightly with a mixture made of 2 T bread crumbs and 2 T Parmesan cheese. Place on baking sheet and bake in 375°F. oven for 25 minutes, or until crusty on top.

Serves 6.


## OLIVE SPREAD

1/2 C butter, softened
2 T milk
2 drops red food coloring
3 T stuffed green olives, chopped

In a small mixer bowl beat the butter, milk, and food coloring. Beat until fluffy. Stir in the olives. Spread on crackers. For variations, use yellow or green food coloring and arrange on serving tray.

*Makes approximately 3/4 cup.*

15

# FLAVORED BUTTER SPREADS

1/2 C butter, softened

Cream butter and add one of the following. Mix thoroughly.

CAVIAR:
    4 T caviar
    1/2 tsp grated onion
    2 tsp lemon juice

CHIVE:
    1/4 C chopped chives
    1/2 tsp Worcestershire sauce

GREEN PEPPER:
    1/4 C green pepper, grated and drained
    1/2 tsp lemon juice

HONEY:
    1/2 C honey

HORSERADISH:
    1/4 C fresh horseradish, grated

LEMON:
    1 tsp lemon rind, grated
    2 T lemon juice

MUSTARD:
    1/4 C prepared mustard

SARDINE:
    1/2 C sardines, skinned, boned, and mashed
    2 T lemon juice
    2 T grated onion

1/2 C cooked shrimp, minced
1/4 tsp garlic salt
1/4 tsp paprika
1 tsp lemon juice

Spread on crackers or wheat rounds.

## JELLIED LIVER AND HAM PATE

3 envelopes (3 T) unflavored gelatin
1 C water
1 can (10-1/2 oz) consomme
3/4 lb braunschweiger or liverwurst
2 cans (4-1/2 oz) deviled ham
1 bottle (12 oz) beer
3/4 tsp thyme
3/4 tsp Tabasco sauce
1/4 tsp black pepper
Parsley, chopped
Lettuce

Soften gelatin in water for 5 minutes. Heat consomme to boiling and add softened gelatin. Stir until dissolved. Blend liverwurst, deviled ham, beer, thyme, Tabasco sauce and pepper. Combine with consomme mixture and stir well. Pour into a 1-1/2-quart mold. Chill until ready to serve. Unmold on bed of lettuce and garnish with chopped parsley.

Serves 12.

# VEGETABLE HORS D'OEUVRES

' ₁g (3 oz) cream cheese
2 T milk
1/2 tsp curry powder
12 3-inch lengths celery
2 T dill, minced
18 cherry tomatoes
1/4 C mayonnaise
3 T chives, minced
2 medium-sized cucumbers
1 can (2 oz) deviled ham
2 T parsley, minced
12 mushroom caps
2 T butter

Soften cream cheese and mix with milk. Divide in half. Add curry powder to half of cream cheese mixture and use to stuff celery pieces. Add dill to remaining half of cream cheese and reserve. Hollow out cherry tomatoes and fill with mixture of mayonnaise and minced chives. Peel cucumbers and slice off each end. Using a sharp knife, remove seeds, making cucumbers into hollow tubes. Stuff with mixture of deviled ham and parsley. Refrigerate for 1 hour. Cut into 1/2-inch slices. Sauté mushroom caps in melted butter. Set aside. Chop stems fine and sauté. Mix with dill cream cheese mixture. Stuff mushroom caps. Refrigerate all until time to serve.

*Serves 6.*

# PATE

2 lbs calves' liver
1/2 lb chicken livers
2 eggs, beaten
1/2 C heavy cream
2 T lemon juice
1 tsp garlic salt
4 T brandy
4 slices bacon, cooked and crumbled

Put livers through finest blade of food grinder. Add all other ingredients except brandy and bacon. Mix well. Warm the brandy in a small saucepan. Ignite and pour over liver mixture when flames subside. Pack liver into a well greased loaf pan. Cover pan tightly with aluminum foil. Place loaf pan in large shallow pan containing 1-1/2 inches of water. Bake in a 325°F. oven for two hours. Remove from oven and remove foil. Weight the pâté with a heavy object that will cover loaf. Chill overnight. Unmold on bed of greens and top with crumbled bacon.

Serves 10 to 12.

## ANTIPASTO ROLLS

1 can (8 oz) pitted black olives
1 jar (4 oz) Italian roasted red peppers
1/4 lb thin sliced Prosciutto

Drain olives and peppers. Cut peppers into 1-inch strips. Lay slice of Prosciutto flat. Center a strip of pepper on each slice of meat. Put olive at one end of meat slice and roll jelly-roll fashion. Fasten with toothpicks.

*Makes about 15 rolls.*

# COCKTAIL MEATBALLS

1 lb lean ground beef
2 T onion, minced
1 C fine cornflake crumbs
1 tsp cornstarch
1/2 tsp salt
1/4 tsp pepper
1/8 tsp allspice
1 C milk
Oil for deep frying

Mix all ingredients except oil thoroughly. Form into small balls about 3/4 of an inch in diameter. Let stand for 15 minutes. Heat oil in frying pan to 375°F. Deep fry meatballs for 1-1/2 to 2 minutes. Drain on absorbent paper. Serve hot with toothpicks.

Makes approximately 60 meatballs.

## HAM AND CHEESE AMERICANA

1/2 C dairy sour cream
1/2 C mayonnaise
1/4 tsp dry mustard
24 slices cold boiled ham
6 slices American cheese, each cut into 4 lengthwise
 strips
24 stuffed olives

Combine dairy sour cream, mayonnaise and mustard. Lay ham slice flat. Spread with some of the sour cream mixture. Lay strip of American cheese on one end of ham slice. Roll jelly-roll fashion. Fasten with toothpick topped with olive.

*Makes 24 rolls.*

## TANGY HAM ROLLUPS

1-1/2 C flour
1-1/2 tsp baking powder
1/2 tsp salt
1 C Cheddar cheese, shredded
1/2 C butter
1/4 C cold water
8 thin slices boiled ham
Mustard

Sift the flour, baking powder and salt into a mixing bowl. Combine with cheese and butter. Gradually add water, stirring with a fork, until dough sticks together. Knead on floured surface 10 times. Divide dough in half and roll out each half on floured surface to a 10 x 14-inch rectangle. Cut each rectangle into four 5 x 7-inch pieces. Place a slice of boiled ham on each piece of dough. Spread lightly with mustard. Roll jelly-roll fashion, starting at the narrow end. Seal edge. Place seam-side down on a greased cookie sheet. Bake in 450°F. oven for 10 to 12 minutes, until golden brown. Remove from oven, cut each roll into 5 or 6 slices and serve while hot.

*Serves 8 to 10*

## CHICKEN PINEAPPLE SPREAD

1/4 C crushed pineapple
1/2 C chicken, cooked and minced
3 T mayonnaise

Drain pineapple and reserve liquid. Combine all ingredients and mix well. Thin mixture to desired consistency with pineapple juice. Spread on crackers or toast squares.

*Makes approximately 1 cup.*

## PERSIAN CANAPES

4 T mayonnaise
16 2-inch rounds of white bread
32 small or medium-sized shrimp, cooked and shelled
1 2-oz jar black caviar
1 hard cooked egg yolk, sieved

Spread mayonnaise lightly on bread rounds. Place 2 shrimp in center of each. Surround with border of caviar and dust lightly with egg yolk. Cover with plastic wrap and refrigerate until ready to serve.

*Makes 16 canapes.*


## WAFFLES A LA RUSSE

1 recipe waffle mix
1/2 C sour cream
1 4-oz jar caviar

Prepare waffle mix as directed on package. Drop batter from a tablespoon on to a greased, heated, waffle iron for small round waffles. Be careful not to let waffles touch. When done, put aside. Just before serving reheat in 350°F. oven for 5 minutes. Top each with sour cream and caviar.

*Makes about 25 small waffles.*

## MUSHROOM PUFFS

1 can (4-1/2 oz) deviled ham
24 assorted crackers
1-1/2 C Cheddar cheese, grated
3/4 C mayonnaise
1 can (4 oz) button mushrooms, drained

Spread ham on crackers and place in broiler pan. In a small mixing bowl combine the cheese and mayonnaise. Spread on top of deviled ham. Top with button mushrooms. Place under broiler for about 1 minute, or until the cheese mixture bubbles and becomes slightly browned.

*Makes 24 puffs.*


## BUBBLY CHEESE AND BACON

1/2 lb bacon, cooked
3/4 C American cheese, shredded
1/4 C butter, softened
Toast rounds

Crumble cooked bacon and mix together with cheese and butter. Spread on toast rounds. Line cookie sheet with aluminum foil. Place rounds on cookie sheet and broil about 4 inches from heat until cheese melts and bubbles. Remove from broiler and serve while still hot.

*Makes about 50 pieces.*

## AVOCADO SPREAD

2 ripe avocados
3 T lemon juice
1/4 tsp salt
1/4 tsp seasoned pepper
2 strips bacon, cooked and crumbled

Peel avocados and mash with lemon juice. Add salt, seasoned pepper and crumbled bacon. Mix well. Use as spread on crackers or rye rounds. May also be used as a dip with chips, pretzels, or fresh carrot sticks or celery.

## SESAME PINWHEELS

1 C flour
1-1/2 tsp baking powder
1/2 tsp salt
1/4 C shortening
1/3 C milk
1/4 C green onions, finely chopped
2 T sesame seeds

Sift the flour, baking powder, and salt into a large mixing bowl. Cut in shortening until particles are the consistency of cornmeal. Add milk and stir just until thoroughly moistened. Roll out dough on floured surface into a 20 x 12-inch rectangle. Sprinkle with green onion and sesame seeds. Roll up, starting with the long edge. Seal edge well. Cut into 1/2-inch slices and place flat on greased cookie sheet. Bake at 450°F. oven for 10 to 12 minutes, or until golden. Serve warm.

*Serves 6 to 8.*

## BLEU CHEESE SQUARES

1 pkg bleu cheese salad dressing mix
2 T onion, grated
2 T butter
1 egg
1 pkg (8 oz) cream cheese
2 C flour
1 tsp salt
3/4 C shortening
6 T cold water

In a small bowl combine salad dressing mix, grated onion, butter, egg and cream cheese. Beat until thoroughly blended. Reserve. In separate bowl sift flour and salt. Cut in shortening until particles are fine. Add cold water, and stir with a fork until dough holds together. Roll out on floured board into a 14 x 20-inch rectangle. Cut into two 10 x 14-inch pieces. Spread cheese filling over one half. Top with other half and cut into 2-inch squares. Bake in 425°F. oven for 12 minutes or until lightly browned. Serve hot.

*Makes 35 pieces.*

## HAM AND CHUTNEY SPREAD

1/2 C cooked ham, minced
1/2 C chutney, minced

Combine ingredients and mix well. Spread on crackers, wheat squares, or bread squares. May also be used to fill celery stalks cut into 1-1/2-inch lengths.

*Makes approximately 1 cup.*

## SALMON SPREAD

1 C salmon, flaked
1/2 C mayonnaise
2 T onion, grated
1 tsp lemon juice

Combine all ingredients and mix well. Spread on your favorite crackers. Fresh vegetables such as celery cut into 1-inch lengths, carrot sticks, mushrooms or cauliflowerettes may also be used.

*Makes approximately 1-1/2 cups.*

## GOLDEN CHEESE ROLLS

1 pkg pie crust mix
2 T sweet Vermouth
1-1/2 C Cheddar cheese, shredded
Paprika

Prepare pie crust mix as directed on package using 2 T Vermouth in place of part of the water. Divide dough in half. Roll each half on floured surface to a 12 x 4-inch rectangle. Sprinkle with cheese. Fold long edges over center, sealing edges and ends. Place seam side down on ungreased cookie sheet. Using sharp knife, cut halfway through rolls at 1-inch intervals. Sprinkle with paprika. Bake at 400°F. for 20 minutes, or until golden brown. Serve hot.

*Makes about 24 pieces.*

## DEVILED HAM AND EGG SPREAD

1 can (4-1/2 oz) deviled ham
1 egg, hard cooked and chopped
1 T mayonnaise
1 T chili sauce
1/2 tsp mustard

Combine all ingredients and mix well. Add more mayonnaise if necessary for easy spreading. Spread on your favorite crackers, bread squares, or toast thins.

*Makes approximately 1 cup.*


## LIPTAUER CHEESE

1 pkg (8 oz) cream cheese, softened
8 oz cottage cheese
1/2 lb butter, softened
3 T paprika
4 tsp grated onion
4 tsp minced parsley
1 tsp garlic salt
1/4 C sour cream

Combine all ingredients in a mixing bowl. Stir until thoroughly blended. Cover and refrigerate until serving time. Serve with assorted crackers or raw vegetables such as celery sticks, carrot sticks or cauliflowerettes.

*Makes approximately 3-1/2 cups.*

# SESAME TARTS

2 T sesame seeds
1 pkg pie crust mix

Combine sesame seeds with pie crust mix. Follow directions on package to make pie crust pastry. Chill for 10 minutes. Roll out to 1/4-inch thickness. Cut into 2-inch rounds, preferably scalloped. Place each round into a small muffin tin, and bake at 400°F. for 15 minutes, or until golden brown. Cool and fill tarts with your favorite filling, spread, or dip.

*Makes about 35.*

# TAMPA BLACK BEAN DIP

1 can (10-1/2 oz) black bean soup
1 medium onion, chopped
1 pkg (8 oz) cream cheese
1 T milk
1/2 tsp garlic salt
1 tsp Worcestershire sauce
2 tsp parsley, minced

Combine all ingredients except parsley in blender. Blend just until smooth. Add more milk if desired to thin mixture. Spoon into serving dish and garnish with parsley. Serve with assorted crackers, pretzels, chips or raw vegetables.

*Makes approximately 2 cups.*

## MARINATED OLIVES SAN ANTONIO

2 cans (5-1/4 oz) pitted ripe olives
2 garlic cloves, minced
2 T minced onion
2 T wine vinegar
3 T olive oil
1/4 tsp salt
Pepper to taste

Drain olives. Place olives in a large jar with screw top. Add other ingredients. Close tightly. Shake jar vigorously. Refrigerate at least overnight. Shake jar several times during refrigeration. These olives will keep in the refrigerator for a week.

## CLAM DIP

1 can (7 oz) minced clams
1 pkg (8 oz) cream cheese, softened
1-1/2 tsp Worcestershire sauce
1/2 tsp garlic salt
2 tsp lemon juice
1 tsp onion juice

Drain broth from minced clams and reserve. Mash cream cheese until soft. Combine with all other ingredients except clam juice. Thin mixture to desired consistency with clam juice. Serve at room temperature. Use your favorite item to dip with.

*Makes approximately 1-1/2 - 2 cups.*

## ZINGY AVOCADO DIP

1-1/2 C celery, diced
1 avocado, peeled and diced
1 C French dressing
1 T prepared horseradish
1 pkg (8 oz) cream cheese, softened
1/3 C sour cream
1 T onion powder
1 tsp garlic salt

Combine all ingredients in blender. Serve with raw vegetables, assorted crackers, or potato chips. May also be served spread on crackers, or celery if desired.

*Makes approximately 3-1/2 cups.*

## PARTY MIX

1 stick margarine
1 T Worcestershire sauce
1 T garlic salt
2 C wheat square cereal
2 C corn square cereal
2 C rice square cereal
1 can (7-1/2 oz) salted peanuts
2 C thin pretzel sticks, broken

Heat oven to 250°F. Melt margarine in a large shallow baking dish. Mix in Worcestershire sauce and garlic salt. Add cereals, peanuts, and pretzels and mix thoroughly. Bake in oven for one hour, stirring every 15 minutes. Cool and store in airtight container.

*Makes about 2 quarts.*

# Chapter 2

# QUICK BREADS

## BUFFET BREAD

1 long loaf French or Italian bread
1/2 C butter
1/4 C parsley, finely chopped
1/4 C green onion, finely chopped

Cut bread lengthwise, but not all the way through. Soften butter and mix in parsley and green onion. Spread mixture in center of the bread. Close bread and wrap in aluminum foil. Bake in a 400°F. oven for 10 minutes or until butter melts. Slice and serve warm.

*Serves 6.*

## THREE GRAIN BREAD

1 C corn meal
1 C rye flour
1 C graham flour
2 tsp baking soda
1 tsp salt
1/8 tsp allspice
3/4 C molasses
1-3/4 C sour milk
1/4 C cream

Put dry ingredients in a large mixing bowl and mix well. In a separate bowl place the molasses, sour milk and cream. Stir until well blended. Pour liquid slowly into dry mixture. Stir only until well moistened. Pour batter into well-greased 9-inch loaf pan and bake in 350°F. oven for 1 hour and 15 minutes, or until done. Cool thoroughly before slicing.

*Serves 12.*

# ITALIAN GARLIC BREAD

1/2 C butter, softened
2 garlic cloves, halved
1/2 C Italian cheese, grated
1 loaf French or Italian bread

Cream butter. Pierce garlic halves with toothpick. Submerge garlic in butter. Let stand for one half hour, stirring occasionally. Remove garlic and add the grated cheese to garlic butter. Slice bread not quite through in 1-inch slices. Spread the slices with the garlic butter. Wrap aluminum foil around bread and bake in hot oven, 400°F., until butter and cheese mixture melts, about 10 minutes. Serve hot.

*Serves 6.*

# HIGHLAND SCONES

2 C flour
4 tsp baking powder
1/2 tsp salt
1/4 C butter, softened
2 eggs, beaten
6 T milk

Sift flour, baking powder and salt twice. Add the butter, eggs and milk. Mix just until thoroughly moistened. Turn onto well floured board and knead 10 times. Roll out 1/2 inch thick. Cut into small rounds, about 2 to 2-1/2 inches. Place on greased cookie sheet and bake in preheated oven at 400°F. for 12 to 15 minutes. Serve with butter and marmalade.

*Makes about 36 scones.*

## GINA'S CRANBERRY NUT LOAF

2 C flour
1 tsp baking soda
1 tsp salt
3 T vinegar, plus water to make a total of 2/3 C
1 egg
3/4 C sugar
1/4 C salad oil
1/3 C orange juice, fresh or frozen     **1817207**
1 tsp grated orange rind
1 C chopped cranberries
1 C nuts, chopped (any kind you choose to use)

Sift together the flour, baking soda and the salt. Pour the 3 tablespoons of vinegar into a measuring cup. Add water to make a measure of 2/3 cup. Beat egg in a large mixing bowl. Add the sugar, oil, vinegar and water mixture, orange juice, and the orange rind. Mix well. Add the dry ingredients and blend thoroughly. Stir in cranberries and nuts. Grease and line a 5 x 9-inch loaf pan with wax paper. Pour the batter into the pan and bake in a 350°F. oven for 50 minutes or until the loaf tests done.

*Serves 12.*

# PLYMOUTH PUMPKIN BREAD

1-1/2 C sugar
1/2 C vegetable oil
2 eggs
1-2/3 C flour
1/2 tsp cinnamon
3/4 tsp salt
1/2 tsp nutmeg
1 tsp baking soda
1/3 C water
1 C cooked pumpkin, mashed
1/2 C walnuts, chopped

Combine sugar and oil in a large mixing bowl. Add eggs, beating well after each addition. Sift dry ingredients together. Add dry ingredients alternately with water to mixture in the mixing bowl. Add pumpkin and fold in the nuts. Pour batter into a well greased 5 x 9-inch loaf pan. Bake in a 350°F. oven for 50 to 60 minutes, or until loaf tests done. Cool thoroughly before slicing.

*Serves 12.*

## CAPE COD BISCUITS

4 C biscuit mix
1-1/2 C milk
16 tsp whole cranberry sauce

Blend biscuit mix and milk with fork just until thoroughly moistened. Drop from spoon onto lightly greased cookie sheet, making 16 biscuits. With the back of a teaspoon make a small depression in the center of each biscuit. Bake in a 450°F. oven for 10 to 15 minutes, or until biscuits are a golden brown. Just before serving fill depressions in top of biscuits with the cranberry sauce.

*Makes 16.*

## LIMPA MUFFINS

1 egg
1 C rye flour
3/4 C flour
1/4 C brown sugar, firmly packed
4 tsp baking powder
1/2 tsp salt
1-1/2 tsp grated orange peel
3/4 C milk
1/4 C cooking oil
1/4 C molasses

Beat the egg slightly in a large mixing bowl. Add all other ingredients. Mix until just thoroughly moistened. Fill well greased muffin cups about one half full. Bake in 400°F. oven for 15 to 20 minutes or until golden brown.

*Makes 12 muffins.*

# ITALIAN BISCUITS

2 C flour
3 tsp baking powder
1 tsp salt
1/3 C shortening
2/3 C American or Cheddar cheese, shredded
2 T green pepper, finely chopped
1 T pimiento, chopped
3/4 C milk

In a large mixing bowl combine the flour, baking powder and salt. Cut in the shortening until particles are fine. Blend in the cheese, pepper, and the pimiento. Mix well. Add milk; mix only until moistened thoroughly. Knead on floured surface 10 times. Roll out to 1/2-inch thickness and cut into rounds with floured 2-1/4-inch cutter. Place on ungreased cookie sheet. Bake at 450°F. for 15 minutes.

*Makes 18 biscuits.*

## APRICOT CRESCENTS

2 pkgs (8 oz) refrigerated crescent rolls
16 tsp apricot jam
2 T butter, melted
2 T sugar
2 T nuts, chopped fine

Take refrigerated crescent rolls from package. Lay flat. Place 1 tsp apricot jam on wide end. Roll up and bake according to directions on package. Brush with melted butter and sprinkle with sugar and chopped nuts. Serve warm.

*Makes 16 rolls.*

# ORANGE NUT MUFFINS

2 C flour
1/3 C sugar
3 tsp baking powder
1 tsp salt
1/2 C hazelnuts, chopped
1 egg
1/2 C orange juice (fresh or frozen)
1 T grated orange peel
1/2 C orange marmalade
1/4 C milk
1/4 C cooking oil

In a large mixing bowl combine flour, sugar, baking powder, salt, and chopped hazelnuts. Combine egg, orange juice, orange peel, orange marmalade, milk, and oil. Add to dry ingredients. Mix only until evenly moistened. Do not overmix. Fill paper lined muffin cups 2/3 full and set aside.

*TOPPING:*

1/4 C sugar
1 T flour
1 T butter, softened
1/2 tsp cinnamon

In a small mixing bowl combine all the topping ingredients. Sprinkle topping over muffin batter. Bake at 400°F. for 20 to 25 minutes, or until muffins are golden brown and test done.

*Makes 12 muffins.*

# CRUNCHY TOAST STICKS

4 slices white bread, toasted
1/3 C corn flake crumbs
1/4 C grated Romano cheese
1/2 tsp onion salt
1/3 C butter, softened

Remove crust from toast slices. Cut each slice into 4 long sticks. Combine corn flake crumbs with cheese. Mix onion salt with butter. Roll each toast stick first in the butter and then in the corn flake-cheese mixture. Just before serving, place on an ungreased cookie sheet and bake in 400°F. oven for 5 minutes, or until crisp.

*Makes 16 sticks.*

# CRUNCHY CARAWAY STICKS

2 C flour
3 tsp baking powder
1 tsp salt
4 T sugar
1/2 C shortening
1 T caraway seeds
3/4 C milk

Sift together the flour, baking powder, salt, and sugar. Cut in the shortening until the mixture is the consistency of cornmeal. Add the caraway seeds and enough milk to give the dough the consistency of a biscuit dough. Knead on a lightly floured board 6 times. Roll out 1/4 inch thick. Cut into strips 4 inches long and 1/4 inch wide. Place on a lightly greased cookie sheet and bake at 375°F. for 10 minutes or until a light brown.

*Makes about 20 sticks.*

## GARLIC BUTTER STICKS

1/3 C butter
2-1/4 C sifted flour
1 T sugar
3-1/2 tsp baking powder
1-1/2 tsp salt
1 C milk
1 tsp garlic salt

Preheat oven to 450°F. Melt butter in a 13 x 9 x 2-inch pan. Remove pan from oven as soon as the butter melts. Sift flour, sugar, baking powder, and salt together. Add milk and stir slowly with a fork until dough just clings together. Turn onto a well floured board and knead lightly 10 times. Roll out 1/2 inch thick into a 12 x 8-inch rectangle. With a floured knife cut the dough in half lengthwise, then crosswise into 1/2-inch strips. Roll each strip in the melted butter and lay close together in two rows in the baking pan. Sprinkle with garlic salt. Bake in the preheated oven at 450°F. for 15 to 20 minutes, until golden brown. Serve hot.

*Makes 32 sticks.*

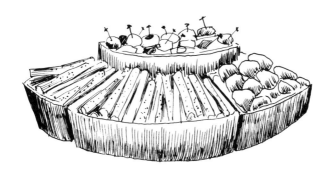

# BLUEBERRY ORANGE BREAD

2-1/4 C flour
3/4 C brown sugar, firmly packed
3 tsp baking powder
1 tsp salt
1/4 C butter, softened
1 egg
2 T orange peel, grated
1/2 C milk
1/4 C orange juice (fresh or frozen)
1 C blueberries (thawed and drained if frozen, cleaned and drained if fresh)

In a large mixing bowl combine all ingredients except the blueberries. Mix at low speed until well blended, then beat at medium speed for 2 minutes. Stir in the blueberries. Turn into a 9 x 5-inch loaf pan, which has been greased on the bottom only. Bake at 350°F. for 60 to 70 minutes, or until bread tests done. Cool 10 minutes, then remove from pan. Cool thoroughly before slicing.

*Serves 12.*

# CHEESE PUFFS

1/2 C water
1/4 C butter
1/4 tsp salt
1/2 C flour
2 eggs
4 oz cream cheese, softened
1 jar (5 oz) process sharp American cheese spread, softened

In a saucepan combine water, butter, and salt. Heat to boiling. Add flour all at once, stirring constantly until the mixture forms a ball and leaves the sides of the pan. Remove from heat. Blend in eggs one at a time, beating vigorously after each addition until the mixture is smooth and glossy. Stir in the softened cheeses until well blended. Drop dough from a teaspoon onto a well greased cookie sheet. Bake at 400°F. for 15 to 20 minutes, or until golden brown. Remove from cookie sheets immediately. Serve either warm or at room temperature.

*Makes 48 puffs.*

## ORANGE WHEAT STICKS

1 C flour
1/2 C wheat germ
2 T sugar
2 tsp baking powder
1/2 tsp salt
2 T grated orange rind
1/3 C milk
1/4 C melted butter
1 egg
2 T orange marmalade

Combine flour, wheat germ, sugar, baking powder, salt, and orange rind in a mixing bowl. Combine milk, melted butter, egg, and orange marmalade. Pour over the dry ingredients and stir just until all the ingredients are moistened. Grease corn-stick pans well. Fill half full with batter. Bake in a 375°F. oven for 15 to 18 minutes, or until sticks test done.

*Makes 12 sticks.*

# TWIST STICKS

1/4 C butter, softened
2 T grated Romano cheese
2 T grated onion
1 T butter
2 C buttermilk biscuit mix
1/2 C milk

Cream together the butter and cheese. Sauté onion in butter until lightly browned and add to butter-cheese mixture. In a separate bowl, combine biscuit mix and the milk. Form dough into a ball. Knead on lightly floured surface 6 times. Roll into a 10 x 12-inch rectangle. Spread with the butter and cheese mixture. Fold into thirds lengthwise, making a rectangle approximately 12 x 3-1/2 inches. Slice into strips 3/4 of an inch wide. Twist each strip in the center and place on ungreased cookie sheet. Bake in a 400°F. oven for 15 minutes, or until lightly browned.

*Makes 16 twists.*


# BACON STICKS

1/2 C American cheese, shredded
6 slices bacon, cooked and crumbled
1/2 tsp onion salt
2 C packaged biscuit mix
3 T bacon drippings

Stir cheese, bacon, and onion salt into dry biscuit mix. Make dough according to package directions for rich biscuits, substituting bacon drippings for shortening. Knead as directed for rolled biscuits. Roll to rectangle 6 x 10 inches. Cut into strips 10 inches long by 1 inch wide. Cut each long strip into thirds crosswise, making 18 sticks. Place 1 inch apart on ungreased baking sheet. Bake in 450°F. oven for 10 minutes.

*Makes 18 sticks.*

## CORN STICKS

2 C cornmeal
3 tsp baking powder
1 tsp salt
1 egg, beaten
1-1/4 C milk
3 T melted butter

Sift together the cornmeal, baking powder, and salt. Mix together the beaten egg, milk and the butter and add to the dry ingredients. Stir just to moisten thoroughly. Pour batter into hot greased corn-stick pans, filling about 2/3 full. Bake at 450°F. for 15 to 20 minutes, or until done.

*Makes 8 sticks.*

# Chapter 3

# SALADS

## ELI'S SALAD NICOISE

1 can (7 oz) white meat tuna fish
1 jar (7 oz) Italian roasted sweet peppers, cut into strips
1 can (4 oz) eggplant caponata
1 can (1 lb) jumbo pitted black olives
1 can (2 oz) flat anchovy fillets, drained
4 eggs, hard cooked and cut into quarters
2 slices red onion, separated into rings

Empty contents of tuna fish can directly onto the center of the serving platter. Arrange remaining ingredients on the platter. Cover with plastic wrap and refrigerate. A half hour before serving, remove from refrigerator and allow to come to room temperature.

*Serves 8 to 10.*

## CONFETTI COLE SLAW

1 small head cabbage, shredded
1 carrot, pared and grated
1 green pepper, chopped
2 T onion, chopped
1/2 C mayonnaise salad dressing
1/4 C milk
2 T sugar
1/4 tsp salt
1/4 tsp seasoned pepper

Toss vegetables together in a salad bowl. In a small mixing bowl combine mayonnaise, milk, sugar, salt, and seasoned pepper. Pour over vegetables and toss lightly until thoroughly mixed.

*Serves 8 to 10.*

# FRENCH TOSSED SALAD

1 head lettuce
1/2 head chickory
1 bunch watercress
3 tomatoes, cut into wedges
1 red onion, thinly sliced
1 cucumber, thinly sliced
1 can (2 oz) flat anchovy fillets, drained
1 C French dressing
1/4 C mayonnaise
1/4 C Roquefort cheese, crumbled

Wash the salad greens and pat dry. Tear into bite-sized pieces and place in a salad bowl. Add tomatoes, onion, and cucumber. Cut anchovy fillets into small pieces and add to salad bowl. In a separate bowl combine the French dressing and mayonnaise. Fold in the cheese and blend well. Just before serving, pour salad dressing over the salad and toss lightly.

*Serves 8.*

# TOSSED BALKAN SALAD

6 C mixed salad greens, torn into bite-sized pieces
1 C plain yogurt
1/4 C French dressing
1/2 tsp garlic salt
1 T sugar

Place greens in a salad bowl. Mix yogurt, French dressing, garlic salt, and sugar in a mixing bowl. Just before serving, pour mixture over the salad greens and toss well.

*Serves 6 to 8.*

# FOUR-WAY VEGETABLE SALAD

3 packages (3 oz each) lemon-flavored gelatin
2-1/4 C boiling water
1-1/2 T white vinegar
1/2 tsp garlic salt
3 C cold water
1 C carrots, shredded
1 C celery, thinly sliced
1/4 C red pepper, diced
1 C green pepper, diced
1 C canned diced beets, well drained

Dissolve gelatin in boiling water. Add vinegar, garlic salt, and cold water. Put into a 2-1/2 quart mixing bowl. Chill. When thickened but not firm, divide into quarters. Section off one quarter with two small plates and mix in the carrots. Move one plate to section off the next quarter and mix in the celery and red pepper. Move plate to section off the third quarter and mix in the green pepper. Move plate to the last quarter and mix in the beets. Chill until firm. Unmold and garnish with parsley and black olives.

*Serves 10.*

# MARINATED MUSHROOMS

1 lb small fresh mushrooms
1/4 C olive oil
3 T lemon juice
1 garlic clove, halved
1/2 tsp salt
1/8 tsp pepper
1/8 tsp oregano

Remove the stems from the mushrooms. Save stems for soups, stews, or to combine with other vegetables. Wipe caps with a paper towel. Put into a jar. Combine the other ingredients in a saucepan and heat just to the boiling point. Pour over the mushrooms. Cool. Cover and refrigerate for at least 2 days. Shake twice a day. When serving, drain and serve with toothpicks.

*Serves 12.*


# GREEN BEAN AND DILL SALAD

3 pkgs (9 oz each) frozen cut green beans
1/3 C salad oil
3 T wine vinegar
2 tsp dill, minced
1/2 tsp salt
1/4 tsp seasoned pepper

Cook frozen green beans as directed on package. Drain. Add remaining ingredients and mix well. Chill until ready to serve.

*Serves 10.*

## CHRISTMAS RELISH TREE

This is a very attractive way to serve raw vegetables and relishes at holiday time.

1 styrofoam cone, 12 inches high
Green foil wrapping
Colored toothpicks
Assorted vegetables and pickles, such as:

    cherry tomatoes
    radishes
    black olives
    tiny cucumber pickles
    button mushrooms
    sweet pickle chunks
    raw cauliflowerettes
    pickled onions
    pickled watermelon rind
    green olives
    sour pickles
    pickled red peppers

Cover styrofoam cone with foil wrapping paper. Decorate with assorted relishes impaled on colored toothpicks. Stand on small plate and garnish with parsley.

# CAESAR SALAD

2 T margarine
1 clove garlic, crushed
1/3 C wheat germ
1/2 C salad oil
1/4 C lemon juice
1/4 C wine vinegar
1 T Worcestershire sauce
1 head iceberg lettuce, torn into bite-sized pieces
1 head Romaine lettuce, torn into bite-sized pieces
2 eggs
1/4 C Parmesan cheese, grated
1 can (2 oz) flat anchovy fillets, drained and chopped
Freshly grated pepper to taste

Melt margarine in a small saucepan. Add garlic and cook over low heat 5 minutes. Stir in wheat germ and set aside. In a small bowl, combine oil, lemon juice, vinegar, and the Worcestershire sauce. Blend well. Place lettuce in a large salad bowl. Break eggs over the lettuce. Just before serving, pour the oil mixture over the lettuce and toss until all traces of egg disappear. Add wheat germ mixture, cheese, anchovy fillets, and the pepper. Toss again until everything is well blended and mixed.

*Serves 8 to 10.*

## CREAMY CARROT COLE SLAW

2 C carrots, grated
2 C cabbage, finely shredded
1/2 C mayonnaise
3 T milk
1/2 tsp celery seed
1 tsp sugar

Mix carrots and cabbage together. In a small mixing bowl mix the mayonnaise, milk, celery seed, and sugar. Toss with mixed vegetables.

*Serves 6 to 8.*


## PICKLED GREEN BEANS

2 cans (1 lb each) French cut green beans, drained
1/2 C onion, chopped
1/2 C wine vinegar
1/4 C salad oil
1 tsp prepared horseradish
1/2 tsp garlic salt
1 T sugar
1/4 tsp allspice
1/4 tsp dry mustard

In a large saucepan combine the beans with the onion. In a screw-top jar combine the vinegar, horseradish, oil, and seasonings. Shake vigorously. Pour over the beans, bring to a boil, and simmer for 5 minutes, stirring occasionally. Place in a covered container and refrigerate until serving time.

*Serves 8.*

# HOT GERMAN POTATO SALAD

10 medium potatoes, boiled in their skins
8 slices bacon, diced
2 medium onions, diced
3/4 C sugar
2 tsp dry mustard
2 eggs, beaten
3/4 C vinegar
Salt to taste
Pepper to taste
4 eggs, hard cooked and sliced
2 T parsley, chopped

Peel and cube the potatoes and put in an ovenware bowl or casserole. Fry bacon. Remove bacon from pan and reserve. Fry onions in bacon fat until tender, but not browned. Mix sugar and mustard together. Add to onions in frying pan. Add the beaten eggs and vinegar to onion mixture and cook until thickened, stirring constantly. Pour over the potatoes. Add salt and pepper to taste. Add reserved bacon and egg slices. Mix lightly. Heat in a 250°F. oven for 30 minutes or until ready to serve. Sprinkle parsley on top.

*Serves 8 to 10.*

## APPLE CIDER SALAD

2 T unflavored gelatin
2-1/2 C clear cider
1/4 tsp salt
1/2 C celery, finely chopped
1/2 C red apples, cored but unpeeled and finely chopped
1 T parsley, finely chopped
1/4 C walnuts, finely chopped

Soak gelatin in 1/2 cup of the cold cider. Heat the remaining cider to the boiling point. Combine with gelatin mixture, add salt, stir and chill. When the gelatin mixture begins to set, stir in the remaining ingredients. Pour into a 1-quart mold and chill until firm.

*Serves 6 to 8.*


## TOMATO ASPIC

2 cans (12 oz each) tangy tomato-vegetable juice
1 T unflavored gelatin
4 T cold water
3 T lemon juice
1 tsp Worcestershire sauce
Salad greens

Heat 1 can of the juice until warm. Soak gelatin in the cold water. Add to warm juice and stir until it dissolves. Add remaining ingredients except salad greens and stir. Pour into 1-quart mold and chill until firm. Just before serving unmold onto bed of crisp salad greens.

*Serves 6 to 8.*

# SUMMER FRUIT SALAD MOLD

2 C hot water
2 pkgs (3 oz each) lemon gelatin
1 C cold water
2 ripe bananas, sliced
1-1/2 C Bing cherries, pitted and halved
4 ripe peaches, peeled and sliced
2 C melon balls (honeydew and/or cantaloupe)
Lettuce
Mayonnaise

Pour hot water over gelatin and stir until dissolved. Add cold water. Pour 3/4 cup gelatin mixture into a lightly oiled 2-quart mold. Chill in refrigerator until it thickens. Cool remaining gelatin mixture to syrup consistency. Arrange some of the fruit in a pattern on the congealed gelatin layer. Add more gelatin mixture. Refrigerate until set. Then add remaining fruit and gelatin mixture. Chill until firm. At serving time unmold onto a bed of lettuce. Serve with mayonnaise to be ladled on the salad.

*Serves 12.*

# WALDORF CHICKEN LOAF

1 envelope (1 T) unflavored gelatin
1/2 C cold chicken stock
3/4 C hot chicken stock
1/2 tsp salt
2 T lemon juice
1/4 C apple, cored but unpeeled, and diced
1-1/4 C cooked chicken, diced
1/2 C celery, diced
Salad greens
1/4 C walnuts

Soften gelatin in cold chicken stock. Add hot stock and salt, and stir until dissolved. Add lemon juice and chill until gelatin begins to thicken. Fold in the apple, chicken and celery. Pour into loaf pan and chill until firm. Unmold on crisp salad greens and garnish with walnuts.

*Serves 8 to 10.*

## SUMMER CHICKEN SALAD

4 C cooked chicken, cubed
1 C celery, sliced
1 pear, peeled, cored and diced
1/3 C mayonnaise
2 T lemon juice
2 tsp grated onion
1 tsp salt
1/4 tsp pepper
Lettuce
1 small cantaloupe, cut up into balls
1/4 lb seedless green grapes
1/4 lb Anjou grapes, cut in half and seeded
1/4 C almonds, slivered

Combine chicken, celery, pear, mayonnaise, lemon juice, onion, salt and pepper. Cover and chill. Break lettuce into bite-sized pieces and line a serving platter. Spoon chicken salad into a ring on the lettuce bed. Fill center of the ring with cantaloupe balls. Garnish the edge with ring of grapes, alternating the anjou and the green. Sprinkle with almonds. Serve icy cold.

*Serves 6 to 8.*

## JELLIED MEAT ASPIC

7 tsp unflavored gelatin
6 T cold water
2 C hot broth or canned consomme
2 tsp onion juice
2 T white vinegar
1 tsp garlic salt
1/2 tsp seasoned pepper
2 C chopped cooked ham, tongue, or poultry
1 C celery, chopped
1/4 C pimiento, diced
Shredded lettuce
Mayonnaise for decorating

Sprinkle gelatin on cold water and soak for 5 minutes. Dissolve in hot broth. Add onion juice, vinegar, garlic salt, and seasoned pepper. Chill until thickened but not firm. Add meat, celery, and pimiento. Pour into loaf pan and chill until firm. When ready to serve, unmold on bed of lettuce and decorate with mayonnaise.

*Serves 8.*


## CHICKEN SALAD TROPICANA

2 C cooked chicken, diced
3/4 C diced celery
1/2 C white grapes, halved
1/2 C French dressing
Salad greens
1 ripe avocado, sliced
1 can (11 oz) Mandarin oranges, drained
18 black olives
1 box cherry tomatoes, or 3 tomatoes, cut into wedges

Combine chicken, celery, grapes, and French dressing. Tear salad greens into bite-sized pieces and arrange on plate. Place chicken salad in the center. Garnish with avocado slices, orange sections, black olives and tomatoes.

*Serves 6 to 8.*

## FIESTA EGGS

1 dozen eggs, hard cooked
2 cans (4-1/2 oz each) deviled ham
4 tsp onion, finely chopped
2 T mayonnaise
1/2 tsp tarragon
6 stuffed green olives, halved
Lettuce

Shell eggs. Cut slice from pointed end of each egg. Remove yolks and mash. Mix yolks with ham, onion, mayonnaise, and tarragon. Fill egg cases with yolk mixture and cover filling with the egg slices. Top each egg with half a green stuffed olive. Serve on a bed of lettuce.

*Serves 12.*

# LOBSTER SALAD ORIENTAL

2 cans (7 oz each) lobster
1 T butter
1 T soy sauce
1 C walnuts
1 C celery, sliced diagonally
1/2 C onions, sliced
1 can (5 oz) water chestnuts, drained and sliced
1 can (11 oz) Mandarin orange segments, drained
Oriental dressing (*see below*)
Salad greens

Remove lobster from can and rinse in cold water. Drain. Break into bite-sized pieces. Melt butter, add soy sauce and walnuts. Stir gently over low heat until walnuts are lightly toasted, about 10 minutes. Remove from heat. Combine celery, onion, water chestnuts, orange segments and lobster. Add just enough oriental dressing to hold ingredients together. Add walnuts. Line serving dish with salad greens and arrange lobster salad on top. Serve with remaining salad dressing in a separate dish.

*Serves 6 to 8.*


# ORIENTAL DRESSING

3 eggs, beaten
1/2 C sugar
2 T flour
1-1/2 tsp garlic salt
1/3 C lemon juice
1/3 C cider vinegar
1 can (14-1/2 oz) evaporated milk
1 T butter, melted

In the top of a double boiler place eggs, sugar, flour, garlic salt, lemon juice, and vinegar. Mix well. Cook over boiling water just until mixture thickens, about 10 minutes. Stir constantly. Remove from heat and beat in evaporated milk and melted butter. Cool, then refrigerate in covered container.

*Makes about 3 cups of dressing.*

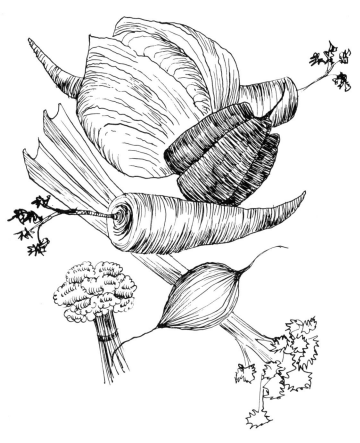

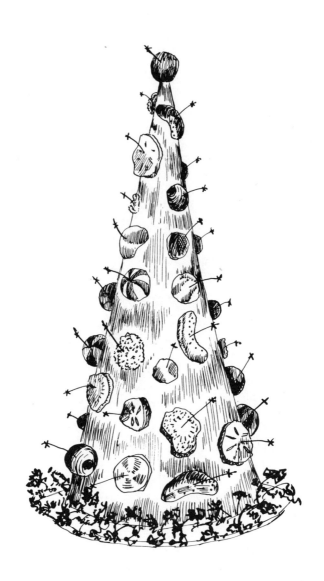

# Chapter 4
# MEAT AND POULTRY

# BEEF WELLINGTON

1 4-lb fillet of beef
Salt to taste
Pepper to taste
4 T butter, softened
1 can (4 oz) chopped mushrooms, drained
2 cans (4 oz each) liver pâté
1/4 tsp rosemary
1 recipe rich or puff paste
1 egg
1 tsp milk

Season beef with salt and pepper. Spread with butter, place in a roasting pan, and roast in a 500°F. oven 25 to 30 minutes for rare. Remove from oven and cool. Meanwhile, combine mushrooms, liver pâté, and rosemary. When beef is cool spread with pâté mixture. Roll out pastry about 1/4 inch thick into a rectangle large enough to wrap beef and have a few inches in reserve. Wrap beef in pastry, trim edges of pastry, moisten with water and seal. Place on aluminum foil lined cookie sheet, seam side down. Brush crust with egg beaten with milk. Roll out trimmed pastry and cut into narrow strips. Lay across dough-wrapped beef in a lattice pattern and brush again with egg mixture. Prick crust. Bake in 450°F. oven for 15 minutes, or until pastry is delicately browned.

*Serves 8 to 10.*

# BEEF CARBONNADE

1/4 C cooking oil
2 lbs lean beef, cut into 1-inch cubes
Salt to taste
Pepper to taste
2 lbs onions, sliced
2 garlic cloves, minced
2/3 C beef stock
1 bottle (12 oz) beer
1 T brown sugar
1 tsp parsley
1 tsp thyme
1 T arrowroot
2 T cold water

Heat oil in a heavy skillet. Brown meat on all sides. Add salt and pepper to taste. Remove meat from skillet to casserole. Brown onions and garlic in skillet, and add to casserole. In saucepan combine stock, beer, brown sugar, parsley, and thyme. Pour over mixture in casserole. Cover tightly and bake in 325°F. oven for 2-1/2 hours. Mix arrowroot with cold water. Stir into casserole and correct seasoning. Heat 15 minutes longer, or until gravy thickens.

*Serves 8.*

# BEEF BOURGUIGNONNE

6 strips bacon, diced
3 lbs lean beef, cut into 1-inch cubes
Salt to taste
Pepper to taste
1/4 C flour
2 T butter
2 carrots, sliced
2 medium onions, sliced
3 C Burgundy red wine
2 C beef stock or consomme
3 cloves garlic, minced
1/4 C butter
1 lb mushrooms, cut into thick slices
2 cans (1 lb each) small white onions, drained
2 T parsley, minced

Fry bacon in large heavy pan until crisp. Reserve. Season meat with salt and pepper and dredge in flour. Fry in bacon fat until well browned. Remove meat. Add 2 T butter to pan drippings. Brown carrots and sliced onions. In large casserole place bacon, beef cubes, carrots, and onion slices. To drippings in pan add wine, stock, and garlic. Stir and heat thoroughly. Pour over meat mixture in casserole. Cover tightly and cook in 325°F. oven for 3 hours until meat is fork tender. In the meantime, melt 1/4 C butter in frying pan and sauté mushrooms for 5 minutes. Add drained onions and heat. Stir mushrooms and onions into casserole, sprinkle with parsley and serve.

*Serves 8 to 10.*

# SPANISH STEAK

1 lemon
1 orange
1/2 C salad oil
1/4 C olive oil
1 clove garlic, split
1 chuck steak, (1-1/2 inches thick)
Salt to taste
Pepper to taste

Cut fruit into 1/4-inch slices and remove seeds. Heat salad oil and olive oil in skillet. Add fruit slices and garlic. Sauté until fruit rind browns slightly, about 5 minutes. Press fruit with back of spoon so juices will run out. Place steak in deep dish and pierce with a fork. Pour hot oil mixture over steak and marinate for about 4 to 5 hours. Grill or pan broil over high heat for 8 to 12 minutes, until crispy brown outside and juicy inside. Season with salt and pepper. Garnish with the fruit slices.

*Serves 6.*

# LATIN AMERICAN PEPPERED STEAK

1 C black pepper, coarsely cracked
1/2 tsp cardamom, ground
1/2 tsp garlic powder
Steak for 6
1 T tomato paste
1 tsp paprika
1 C soy sauce
1/2 C vinegar

Mix black pepper, cardamom, and garlic powder. One hour before broiling, rub mixture into steak on both sides. Mix together the tomato paste, paprika, soy sauce and vinegar. Broil steaks to desired doneness, but 5 minutes before they are finished remove from grill and coat both sides with tomato paste mixture. Baste them again just as they are removed from the grill. Serve with any additional sauce if desired.

*Serves 6.*

## BUFFET BEEF STEW

3 T butter
2 lbs beef, cut into 1-inch squares
2 medium onions, peeled and chopped
1/2 tsp celery salt
2 T parsley, minced
2 cans (10-1/2 oz) beef consomme
1-1/2 C water
3 carrots, cut into 1-inch pieces
3 stalks celery, cut into 1-inch pieces
3 potatoes, peeled and quartered
3 T flour
1 pkg (10 oz) frozen small peas

Melt the butter in a Dutch oven and brown the beef. Add onions and sauté until onions are golden. Add the celery salt, parsley, one can of consomme and one cup of water. Simmer for one hour, stirring occasionally. Add the second can of consomme and simmer one more hour. Add carrots, celery, and potatoes. Simmer for a half hour longer. To the half cup of water add flour and stir until smooth. Pour the flour mixture into the stew and blend well. Add the frozen peas and continue cooking just until peas are done.

*Serves 6 to 8.*

## HAM AND CHERRIES MOUNT VERNON

1 6-lb rolled, boneless fully cooked ham (a 5 lb canned
    ham may be used)
1 can (1 lb, 5 oz) prepared cherry pie filling
2 T vinegar

Bake ham in 325°F. oven for 30 minutes. Remove
ham from oven and cut away skin with a sharp knife.
Score fat. Combine cherry pie filling and vinegar. Spread
one-third of this mixture over ham and return to oven for
10 minutes. Baste second third of mixture over ham and
return to oven for another 10 minutes. Spread remaining
third of the mixture over ham and leave in oven for an additional 10 minutes, a total of 30 minutes baking time after sauce is put on ham.

*Serves 8 to 10.*

## VIENNA EGGS

10 eggs, hard cooked
2 C cooked ham, diced
2 C cooked potatoes, diced
2 cans (10-1/2 oz) condensed cream of mushroom soup
1/2 C milk
1-1/2 tsp Worcestershire sauce
3 T fresh parsley, chopped
Salt to taste
Pepper to taste

Shell eggs and cut in half lengthwise. Place in a 9 x 13-
inch buttered baking dish, cut side up. Put ham and potatoes around eggs. Combine remaining ingredients and
pour carefully into baking dish. Bake in moderate
350°F. oven for 30 minutes.

*Serves 8.*

## MONTEREY MEAT PIE

1 8- or 9-inch unbaked pastry shell

*FILLING:*

1 egg
1 lb lean ground beef
1 can (7 oz) corn with sweet peppers, well drained
1/2 C cracker crumbs
1/2 C chili sauce
2 T onion, finely chopped
1/2 tsp oregano

Beat egg slightly in mixing bowl. Add beef, corn and peppers, cracker crumbs, chili sauce, onion, and oregano. Mix well. Press meat mixture into pastry-lined pie pan. Bake at 425°F. for 20 minutes.

*TOPPING:*

6 slices bacon, cooked crisp
1 egg
2 T milk
1/2 tsp salt
1/2 tsp dry mustard
1/2 tsp Worcestershire sauce
1 C Monterey Jack cheese, grated

While filling is baking, cook bacon crisp. Combine egg, milk, salt, mustard, Worcestershire sauce, and grated cheese. Mix well. Spread over baked filling. Top with crumbled bacon. Bake an additional 5 minutes, or until cheese melts.

*Serves 6 to 8.*

# SHANGHAI BEEF

3 T peanut oil
1-1/2 lbs beef, cut into 3/4-inch cubes
1 medium onion, sliced
1 clove garlic, minced
1/4 lb mushrooms, sliced
2 stalks celery, cut into 1-inch pieces
2 beef bouillon cubes
1 C boiling water
1 can (5 oz) water chestnuts, drained and cut in half
2 T soy sauce
1 tsp cornstarch
1 T sugar

Heat oil in skillet. Lightly brown beef cubes. Add sliced onion, garlic, mushrooms, and celery and sauté until onions are golden. Dissolve beef bouillon cubes in boiling water. Add bouillon and water chestnuts to beef mixture. Bring mixture to a boil. Mix soy sauce, cornstarch and sugar together, add to beef mixture. Cook over low heat, stirring occasionally, until sauce thickens.

*Serves 6.*

# RUTH'S COMPANY CASSEROLE

4 C noodles (1/2 lb)
1 lb lean ground chuck
2 cans (8 oz) tomato sauce
1/2 lb cottage cheese
1 pkg (8 oz) cream cheese
1/4 C sour cream
1/3 C scallions, minced
2 T butter, melted

Cook noodles according to package directions. Drain. Sauté chuck in skillet until browned, separating with a fork. Stir in tomato sauce. Remove from heat. Combine cottage cheese, cream cheese, sour cream, and scallions. Spread half of the noodles in a 2-quart casserole, and cover with cheese mixture, then cover with remaining noodles. Pour melted butter over the noodles. Pour tomato and meat sauce over all. Bake in 375°F. oven for 45 minutes.

*Serves 8.*

## CALLAHAN STEW

1 lb lean lamb, cut in cubes
2 T flour
1/2 tsp salt
1/4 tsp pepper
2 T cooking oil
1 onion, sliced
Water to cover
1/4 tsp tarragon
2 medium potatoes, diced
4 small carrots, diced
1 small turnip, diced
1 T parsley, chopped

Dust meat with flour, salt and pepper. Heat oil in a heavy pan. Brown the lamb and onions. Add water to cover and the tarragon. Cover pan and cook over low heat until meat is almost done, about 1-1/2 hours. Add the potatoes, carrots and turnip and cook until vegetables are tender, about 20 to 30 minutes longer. Add more water if necessary. Just before serving, add parsley.

*Serves 4 to 6.*

# CURRY MEATLOAF WITH CHEESE SAUCE

2 C flour
1 T baking powder
1/2 tsp salt
1/2 tsp curry powder
1/2 C water
1/4 C cooking oil
2 T catsup
Milk (for brushing)

Combine flour, baking powder, salt, and curry powder in mixing bowl. Combine water, oil, and catsup and add to dry ingredients stirring until dough clings together. Knead lightly on floured surface. Roll out to a 9 x 12-inch rectangle.

*FILLING:*

1 lb lean ground beef
1 can (4 oz) mushroom pieces, drained
1 can (10-3/4 oz) condensed Cheddar cheese soup
3 T flour
2 T minced onion
1 tsp salt
1/4 tsp garlic powder

Combine ground beef, mushrooms, 1/2 cup cheese soup, flour, onion, salt, and garlic powder in mixing bowl. Place filling lengthwise down the center of dough. Bring each edge over the filling and seal. Place seam side down on foil covered cookie sheet. With a sharp knife make diagonal slashes 1-1/2 inches apart through crust, just to the filling. Brush with milk, and bake at 375°F. for 45 minutes. Cut into slices and serve with cheese sauce.

*CHEESE SAUCE:*

1/3 C milk
1 T catsup
Remainder of canned cheese soup

Blend all ingredients in saucepan and heat to boiling point. Ladle over sliced meat loaf.

*Serves 6 to 8.*


## BROILED HAM STEAK FLAMBE


2 ham steaks, 1 to 1-1/2 inches thick
8 T brown sugar
1 T dry mustard
2/3 C orange juice
8 slices orange
8 T orange liqueur

Slash edges of ham steaks and put them in a shallow flameproof serving dish. Combine 4 T brown sugar, mustard, and orange juice. Spread half of this mixture on top of ham. Broil until brown, about 10 minutes. Turn steaks and spread with other half of orange juice mixture. Broil 5 minutes. Arrange orange slices on top of ham. Sprinkle with remaining 4 T brown sugar and broil until done. Just before serving warm liqueur. Pour over ham steaks at the buffet table and ignite.

*Serves 8.*

# HAM AND CHICKEN PIE

1 broiler chicken (about 3-1/2 lbs) cut up
1/4 C celery tops
2-1/2 tsp salt
1/4 C onion, minced
2-1/2 C water
1/2 C butter
1/2 C flour
1/8 tsp pepper
1/2 tsp tarragon
1 can (1 lb) whole boiled onions
2 C cooked ham, cubed
Single crust pastry for cover

In a saucepan combine chicken, celery tops, 2 tsp salt, onion, and water. Heat to boiling, cover, and simmer for 30 minutes or until chicken is tender. Remove chicken from broth and cool. Strain broth and measure 2-1/2 cups (add water if necessary). When chicken is cool enough to handle remove meat from bones and dice. Melt butter in saucepan. Blend in flour, remaining 1/2 tsp of salt, and the pepper. Cook, stirring constantly, until it reaches the boiling point. Stir in the chicken broth and tarragon and continue cooking, stirring, until mixture thickens. Remove from heat and add drained onions, diced chicken, and ham. Place chicken mixture in shallow 10 cup baking dish. Top with pastry and flute around edge, sealing edge of pastry to baking dish. Slit top to let steam escape. Bake in 400°F. oven 40 minutes until pastry is golden.

*Serves 8 to 10.*

# VITELLO TONATO

4 C water
1 C dry white wine
1 onion, quartered
2 cloves
2 stalks celery, cut into 1-inch pieces
2 carrots, cut into 1-inch pieces
4 T chopped parsley
1 tsp salt
1/2 tsp pepper
1 2-lb boned leg of veal, rolled and tied

In a deep heavy pan combine the water, wine, onion, cloves, celery, carrots, parsley, salt and pepper. Bring to a slow boil and add the veal. Add hot water if necessary to cover the veal. When water reaches a boil again, cover and simmer for 1-1/2 hours. Remove from broth, cool to room temperature and refrigerate. Strain broth and save to use as stock in gravies, soups etc.

1 can (7 oz) white meat tuna fish, drained
4 flat anchovy fillets
1/4 C olive oil
1/4 C vegetable oil
6 T lemon juice
6 stuffed green olives, sliced in half

Process tuna, anchovy fillets, oils, and lemon juice in blender until smooth. Slice the cooled veal very thin and arrange on a serving dish. Pour sauce over the veal and refrigerate. Just before serving, garnish with the sliced olives.

*Serves 8.*

# APPLE GLAZED HAM LOAF

*HAM LOAF:*

2 lbs lean pork, ground
1 lb ham, ground
1 medium onion, chopped
1/2 C celery, chopped
2 eggs
1/2 C evaporated milk
1/4 tsp black pepper
1/2 C dry bread crumbs

Mix all ham loaf ingredients well and form into a loaf. Place in roasting pan and bake in 350°F. oven for 1 hour. Remove from oven.

*GLAZE TOPPING:*

1/2 C apple juice
1 tsp cornstarch
1/4 tsp allspice
2 T brown sugar
1 large firm apple

In a small saucepan combine apple juice, cornstarch, allspice and sugar. Heat and stir until sugar melts and mixture thickens slightly. Core and slice the apple. Arrange slices on top of the ham loaf. Pour glaze over the apples and ham loaf and bake an additional half hour in 350°F. oven. Cool thoroughly before serving.

*Serves 8.*

## ROAST VEAL DANUBE

1 4-lb boned veal roast, rolled and tied
6 slices bacon
1 tsp salt
1/2 tsp pepper
1/2 C melted butter
1/2 C white wine

Place meat on rack in roasting pan. Cover top with bacon strips. Sprinkle with salt and pepper. Roast in 325°F. oven for 2 hours, basting frequently with mixture of butter and wine.

*Serves 8.*


## RHONE PORK CHOPS

1 lb sauerkraut
1 jar (15 oz) applesauce
1 T brown sugar
1/4 C white wine
8 loin pork chops, 1 inch thick

Drain sauerkraut and rinse in cold water. Drain again and mix with applesauce and sugar. Place in bottom of shallow baking dish. Sauté pork chops until golden brown on both sides. Arrange on top of sauerkraut mixture in casserole. Pour wine over chops. Cover tightly with aluminum foil and bake in 350°F. oven for 1 hour.

*Serves 8.*

# FLORIDA BROILED CHICKEN

4 chicken breasts, halved
2 tsp salt
1 tsp pepper
1 tsp paprika
Juice of 1 lemon
4 tsp salad oil
1 tsp tarragon

Sprinkle chicken with salt, pepper, and paprika. Place chicken, skin side down, in broiler pan. Combine lemon juice, salad oil and tarragon. Brush half of this mixture over the chicken. Broil 30 minutes in broiler with temperature set at 350°F. and pan 3 to 4 inches from heat, or, set control for broil and place pan 7 to 8 inches from heat. Baste chicken occasionally with pan juices. Turn chicken and brush with remaining lemon mixture. Broil 15 to 30 minutes longer, basting occasionally, until done.

*Serves 8.*


# CHICKEN BREASTS TARRAGON

6 T butter
1 medium onion, chopped
4 large chicken breasts, boned and halved
1 tsp garlic salt
2 tsp dry tarragon
1/4 C dry white wine

Melt butter in a large skillet. Add chopped onion and chicken, skin side down. Sauté until chicken is lightly browned. Turn and sauté other side, adding more butter if necessary. Transfer chicken pieces to casserole. Add garlic salt, tarragon and wine to pan juices. Heat, stirring constantly, just to boiling point. Pour over chicken in casserole, cover tightly, and bake in 400°F. oven for 30 minutes.

*Serves 8.*

## DENNIS' CHICKEN POPOVER

4 T flour
1 tsp garlic salt
1 tsp paprika
1/4 tsp pepper
1 broiler, cut into 8 pieces
3 T bacon drippings
1 pkg popover mix
2 eggs (*per popover directions*)
1-1/4 C milk (*per popover directions*)

Combine flour, garlic salt, paprika and pepper in a bag. Shake chicken pieces, a few at a time, to coat lightly with flour mixture. Melt bacon drippings in heavy frying pan and brown chicken pieces, adding more bacon drippings if necessary. Drain on paper towels. Grease shallow casserole. Prepare popover mix according to package directions. Pour batter into casserole. Put browned chicken pieces into the casserole, standing on edge, so all will fit. Bake in a 450°F. oven 1 hour, or until puffed and golden. (*Do not open oven door.*)

*Serves 4.*

*Note:* If increasing this recipe do not bake in larger casserole, but make two separate dishes.

# CHICKEN FRICASSEE

2 broilers, cut into serving pieces
2 C water
1 onion
2 whole cloves
1 stalk celery
1-1/2 tsp salt
1/4 tsp pepper
1/4 tsp thyme
1/4 C cold water
3 T flour
2 egg yolks
2 T lemon juice
1 tsp sugar
Parsley sprigs
1 lemon, sliced thin

In a large saucepan place chicken, water, onion, cloves, celery, salt, pepper, and thyme. Cover tightly. Bring to a boil and then simmer over low heat 40 minutes. Remove chicken. Strain broth and return two cups to saucepan. Make a paste of 1/4 cup cold water and flour. Add to broth and stir until smooth. Heat to boiling point. Beat together the egg yolks, lemon juice, and sugar. Stir in a small amount of the hot broth. Add egg yolk mixture gradually to broth in saucepan, stirring constantly. Add chicken to sauce and heat thoroughly. Do not boil. Pour into serving dish and garnish with parsley and lemon slices.

*Serves 8 to 10.*

# CHICKEN AND WILD RICE CASSEROLE

1 pkg (6 oz) long grain wild rice
1/4 C butter
1/3 C onion, chopped
1/3 C flour
1 tsp salt
1/4 tsp pepper
1 C half-and-half cream
1 C chicken broth
2 C cooked cubed chicken
1/4 C fresh parsley, minced
1/4 C almonds, chopped

Cook rice according to directions on package. Melt butter in frying pan. Sauté onions until golden. Add flour, salt and pepper to onions. Mix well. Gradually add cream and chicken broth, stirring constantly. Cook until thickened. To cooked rice add the sauce, chicken, parsley, and almonds. Mix well and pour into a greased casserole. Bake in a 425°F. oven for 30 minutes.

*Serves 8.*

# SESAME DRUMSTICKS

6 T butter
1 egg
1/2 C milk
1/2 C flour
1 tsp salt
1/4 tsp pepper
1/4 C sesame seeds
1/4 tsp ginger
12 chicken drumsticks

Preheat oven to 375°F. Melt butter in large shallow baking dish. In a small bowl, beat egg slightly and add milk. In separate bowl combine flour, salt, pepper, sesame seeds and ginger. Dip drumsticks in egg mixture, then in sesame mixture. Roll in melted butter in baking dish. Bake in 375°F. oven for 1-1/2 hours or until crisp and tender.

*Serves 6.*

# CHICKEN TETRAZZINI

1 pkg (8 oz) thin spaghetti
1 can (10-1/2 oz) condensed cream of chicken soup
1/2 C milk
2 C diced cooked chicken
1 can (4 oz) sliced mushrooms
1/4 C grated Parmesan cheese

Cook spaghetti as directed on package. Drain and place in a buttered 2-quart casserole. Mix soup and milk. Add diced chicken and drained mushrooms. Combine chicken mixture with spaghetti. Sprinkle cheese on top. Bake in a 350°F. oven for 30 minutes.

*Serves 6 to 8.*

## TURKEY ROLL WITH STUFFING CASSEROLE

1 boned turkey roll (5 to 7 lbs)
1/4 C Chinese-style sparerib or duck sauce

Place turkey roll in small roasting pan and roast according to package directions. One hour before turkey is finished baste with Chinese-style sauce. Serve with stuffing casserole (below).

*Serves 8 to 10.*

## STUFFING CASSEROLE

1 stick margarine
1/2 C onion, minced
1/2 C celery stalks and leaves, chopped
4 C plain white bread cubes
1 egg
Milk (to make 1/2 cup with egg)
2 T salt
1/2 tsp pepper
1 tsp poultry seasoning (or more to taste if desired)

Melt margarine in large frying pan. Sauté onions and celery until golden. Add half of the bread cubes to frying pan and heat. Beat egg slightly in measuring cup. Add milk to measure one half cup. Mix well. Place remaining half of bread cubes in large mixing bowl. Sprinkle seasonings on dry bread cubes. Add egg mixture and contents of frying pan. Toss lightly. Put in large greased casserole, cover and bake in oven with turkey for the last hour.

*Serves 8 to 10.*

# VEAL SCALLOPS IN CREAM SAUCE

1/3 C flour
1 tsp salt
1/2 tsp pepper
1 tsp paprika
2 lbs veal, cut into scallops
1/4 C butter
3/4 C white wine
1 C light cream

Combine flour, salt, pepper, and paprika. Dredge veal scallops in flour mixture. Melt butter in frying pan and brown veal lightly. Pour in wine and simmer until wine has almost evaporated. Pour in cream and simmer gently, covered, for 20 minutes longer. Transfer meat to serving dish. Pour sauce over meat and serve.

*Serves 6 to 8.*

# Chapter 5
# SEAFOOD

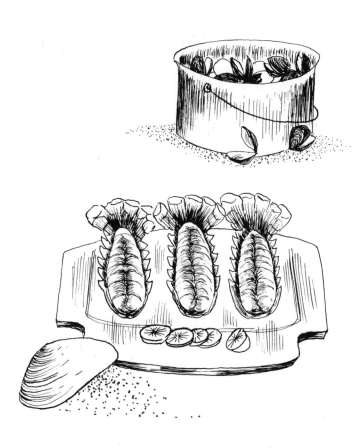

# PAELLA

1/4 C olive oil
1 broiler (about 3 lbs), cut into serving pieces
1 garlic clove, minced
6 strands saffron
1-1/2 C raw long grain rice
1/2 lb pepperoni, sliced in 1/4-inch slices
1 large onion, chopped
1 sweet red pepper, diced
1 green pepper, diced
1 can (14 oz) chicken broth
2 cans (7 oz each) minced clams
1 tsp salt
1 lb raw shrimp, shelled, cleaned and deveined
4 large ripe tomatoes, peeled and cut into eighths
1 pkg frozen peas, defrosted
12 fresh mussels, scrubbed, in shell (optional)

Heat olive oil in large frying pan. Brown the chicken pieces and the garlic. Remove and set aside. Stir in the saffron and rice. Sauté, stirring constantly, until the rice is a golden brown. Add the pepperoni slices, onion, red pepper, and the green pepper. Sauté 7 minutes longer. Stir in the chicken broth, clams and the liquid from both cans of clams, and salt. Cover and let cook for 10 minutes. Meanwhile, in a 3-quart casserole arrange layers of chicken, shrimp, tomatoes and peas. Add the rice and pepperoni mixture. Cover tightly and bake in a 375°F. oven for 1 hour, or until the rice is tender. Remove cover, add mussels, recover and continue baking until shells open.

*Serves 6 to 8.*

## SEAFOOD NAPOLEON

2 pkgs (9 oz each) frozen artichoke hearts
2 C instant rice
1-1/2 lb cooked shrimp or lobster
2 cans (10-1/2 oz each) condensed cream of mushroom
    soup
2-2/3 C water
1 T lemon juice
1/2 tsp dill
1/2 tsp salt
1/4 tsp garlic powder
1 lemon, cut into 8 wedges, for garnish
Parsley for garnish

Cook artichoke hearts as directed on package. Drain
and combine with rice and seafood in a 3-quart casserole.
Mix remaining ingredients except lemon and parsley and
pour into the casserole. Cover and bake in a 400°F. oven
for 35 minutes, or until most of the liquid is absorbed.
Stir before serving. Garnish with lemon wedges and
parsley.

*Serves 8.*

## BASS IN BEER SAUCE

4 T butter
2 large onions, minced
2 T flour
1 bottle (12 oz) beer
1 tsp salt
2 T brown sugar
1/2 tsp black pepper
1 tsp Worcestershire sauce
3 lbs bass, cut into serving-sized pieces
Parsley sprigs for garnish

Melt butter in a large frying pan. Add the chopped onion and sauté until golden brown. Add the flour and cook, stirring constantly, for 2 minutes. Add the beer, salt, brown sugar, pepper, and Worcestershire sauce. Boil, stirring constantly, until sauce thickens slightly. Add fish pieces and cook until fish flakes easily. Transfer fish carefully to serving dish. Pour beer sauce over the fish and garnish with the parsley sprigs.

*Serves 6.*


## SEAFOOD IN PATTY SHELLS

4 cans (10-1/2 oz each) frozen shrimp soup
1-1/2 C milk
1/4 C sherry wine
6 C mixed cooked seafood (flounder, cod, scallops, shrimp, crabmeat, lobster)
Paprika

Defrost soup according to directions on can. Mix soup, milk and sherry in a saucepan. Cut seafood into bite-sized pieces, and add to the soup mixture. Heat just to the boiling point and serve in patty shells (below). Dust lightly with paprika.

## PATTY SHELLS

2 pkgs frozen patty shells, or 12 ready baked

Bake and prepare according to directions on package. Fill with seafood mixture and serve hot.

*Serves 12.*

# DOWN EAST CASSEROLE

1/2 lb lobster
1/2 lb crabmeat
1 lb shrimp, cleaned and deveined
1/2 C green pepper, finely chopped
1/4 C onion, minced
1-1/2 C celery, finely chopped
1 C mayonnaise
1 T Worcestershire sauce
1 tsp salt
2 C potato chips, crumbled

Cut seafood into bite-sized pieces. Place in a large bowl and add chopped pepper, onion, and celery. Mix the mayonnaise, Worcestershire sauce, and salt together in a separate bowl and then pour over the seafood mixture, and mix well. Pour into a 2-quart casserole and top with crumbled potato chips. Bake at 400°F. for 20 to 25 minutes.

*Serves 8.*

# CRABMEAT ST. JACQUES

1 lb. frozen Alaskan King crabmeat, thawed and drained
5 T butter
1 lb fresh mushrooms, sliced
1 C dry white wine
1/2 tsp salt
1/4 tsp pepper
3 T flour
1 C light cream
3/4 C soft bread crumbs

Separate thawed crabmeat into bite-sized chunks. Discard any shell and cartilage. In a heavy saucepan melt 2 tablespoons of butter. Sauté sliced mushrooms until golden brown. Add the crabmeat, wine and seasonings to the mushrooms. Cover and simmer for 10 minutes. Drain, reserving 1 cup of broth. Melt the remaining 3 tablespoons of butter. Add flour, and stir until smooth. Gradually add broth and cream. Bring just to the boiling point, stirring constantly. Add mushrooms and crabmeat to the sauce. Pour into buttered casserole and top with buttered bread crumbs. Bake in a 400°F. oven for 10 minutes, or until lightly browned.

*Serves 8 to 10.*

## BROILED SALMON WITH DILL

3 1-inch thick salmon steaks
2 T butter
1/4 C white wine
1 tsp dill
6 lemon wedges

Cut salmon steaks in half. Arrange the salmon pieces in a flameproof pan. Melt the butter in a small saucepan. Add the wine and dill. Baste salmon with one half of the butter-dill mixture. Broil 10 minutes. Turn steaks and pour on remaining butter-dill mixture. Broil for an additional 5 minutes, or until salmon flakes easily. Serve with the lemon wedges.

*Serves 6.*

## SALMON CASSEROLE

4 C potatoes, peeled and sliced
4 eggs, hard cooked and sliced
1 can (16 oz) salmon, drained and flaked
1 can (10-1/2 oz) condensed cream of mushroom soup
1/2 C milk
2 T parsley flakes
1/2 tsp salt
1/2 tsp Worcestershire sauce
1/2 tsp onion salt

In a greased 2-quart casserole, place half of each in the following order: potato slices, egg slices and salmon. Repeat with the remaining half in the same order. In a mixing bowl, combine the mushroom soup, milk, parsley flakes, salt, Worcestershire sauce and onion salt. Pour over ingredients in the casserole. Cover and bake at 350°F. for 1 hour. Remove cover and bake uncovered for an additional 30 minutes, or until the potatoes test done.

*Serves 8.*


## STUFFED LOBSTER TAILS

12 frozen rock lobster tails
4 T butter
1/2 lb fresh mushrooms
1 T onion, chopped
1 T parsley, chopped
1 C soft bread crumbs
2 T white wine
1/2 tsp salt
1/4 tsp pepper

Parboil frozen lobster tails as directed on package. Cut away soft undershell, split meat. Melt the butter in a heavy skillet. Remove stems from the mushrooms and chop them. Sauté the chopped mushroom stems, onion, and the parsley for 5 minutes. Slice the mushroom caps and add to the mixture in the skillet. Add the bread crumbs, wine, salt and pepper and sauté for 3 minutes longer. Fill the lobster tails with the stuffing mixture and place remaining mixture on the top of the tails. Bake in a preheated 350°F. oven for 15 minutes.

*Serves 6.*

## TUNA SALAD MOLD

2 pkgs (3 oz each) flavored gelatin
1/2 C cold water
2 tsp salt
3 C boiling water
4 T vinegar
2 cans (7 oz) tuna, drained and flaked
2 tsp onion powder
4 T celery, chopped
4 T green pepper, chopped
Mixed salad greens

Soften gelatin in cold water. Add salt and the boiling water and stir until dissolved. Add the vinegar. Chill until thickened. Fold in the remaining ingredients, except salad greens, and pour the mixture into a greased 9 x 5-inch loaf pan. Chill until firm. Unmold on a bed of crisp mixed salad greens.

*Serves 8 to 10.*

# TOSSED TUNA SALAD

2 cans (7 oz) white meat tuna, flaked
1 small head lettuce, torn into bite-sized pieces
2 stalks celery, diced
6 eggs, hard-cooked and sliced
3 tomatoes, cut into wedges
1 small red onion, sliced into rings
1 cucumber, sliced thin
1 tsp mixed salad herbs
Salt to taste
Pepper to taste
2/3 C French dressing

In a large salad bowl combine the tuna, lettuce, celery, sliced eggs, tomatoes, onion rings, cucumber and the salad herbs. Add the salt and pepper to taste. Just before serving add the French dressing and toss until completely mixed.

*Serves 8 to 10.*

# CRAB DELIGHT

1 pkg (10 oz) frozen chopped spinach
1 can (10-1/2 oz) condensed cream of mushroom soup
1/4 C flour
1/2 C milk
1/2 tsp nutmeg
1 can (4 oz) mushroom pieces, drained
1 C Swiss cheese, shredded
2 cans (7-1/2 oz) crabmeat, drained and flaked, any shell
    and cartilage discarded
1/4 C almonds, diced
1/4 C white wine
4 T butter
1-1/2 C bread cubes

Cook spinach as directed on package, and then drain well. Spread spinach in bottom of a 2-quart casserole. In a saucepan, combine soup, flour, milk, and nutmeg. Add the mushrooms. Cook over medium heat until thickened, stirring constantly. Add the Swiss cheese and stir until melted. Add the crabmeat, almonds and the white wine. Pour this mixture over the spinach in the casserole. Melt the butter in a small pan. Combine the butter with the bread cubes and sprinkle on top of the casserole mixture. Bake at 400°F. for 25 minutes, or until the bread cubes are a toasted golden brown.

*Serves 6 to 8.*

# CRABMEAT BISCUIT BAKE

1/2 C green pepper, chopped
1/2 C onion, chopped
1/4 C butter
1/4 C flour
1 tsp dry mustard
1 can (1 lb) tomatoes
1 T Worcestershire sauce
2 pkgs (6 oz) frozen crabmeat, thawed and drained, any
    shell and cartilage discarded
1 C American cheese, shredded
1/4 C sherry
1 can packaged refrigerator biscuits

Sauté green pepper and onion in butter in a saucepan until tender. Blend in the flour and the dry mustard. Gradually stir in the tomatoes and Worcestershire sauce. Cook over medium heat until mixture boils and thickens. Add crabmeat, and simmer covered for 10 minutes. Stir in the cheese and sherry. Pour into a 2-quart casserole. Open the can of biscuits, separate each biscuit and cut into quarters. Arrange on top of the casserole mixture with the points facing up. Bake at 375°F. for 20 to 25 minutes or until biscuits are done.

*Serves 8.*

# CRAB LOUIS

1 head iceberg lettuce
3 C crabmeat, cooked and cleaned
1 ripe avacado, peeled and cut into slices
1 jar (6 oz) marinated artichoke hearts
3 tomatoes, cut into eighths
1 lemon, cut into 6 wedges
6 eggs, hard cooked and cut in half

Tear lettuce into bite-sized pieces and make a bed on 6 individual plates. Arrange crabmeat, cartilage removed, in center of each plate. Divide avacado slices and artichoke hearts evenly between each plate. Garnish each portion with tomato wedges, 1 lemon wedge, and 2 egg halves. Just before serving make *Louis Salad Dressing* (below).

## LOUIS SALAD DRESSING

1/2 C heavy cream
1 C mayonnaise

Whip heavy cream until stiff and then fold in the mayonnaise. Pour salad dressing over each individual salad and serve immediately.

*Serves 6.*

# SALMON SALAD MOLD

1 T (1 envelope) unflavored gelatin
2 T cold water
1/2 T flour
1-1/2 T sugar
1 tsp salt
1 tsp dry mustard
1/4 tsp pepper
2 eggs
3/4 C milk
1/4 C vinegar
1-1/2 T melted butter
1-1/2 C flaked salmon
1/2 C heavy cream, whipped
8 large pitted black olives, halved

Soften gelatin in the cold water. Mix the flour, sugar, salt, dry mustard and pepper in the top of a double boiler. Add the eggs and stir until well blended. Gradually add milk and vinegar. Cook over hot water until the mixture thickens, stirring constantly. Add butter and the softened gelatin and stir until the gelatin is dissolved. Remove from heat. Stir in the salmon. Chill, stirring occasionally. When mixture starts to thicken, fold in the whipped cream and pour into a mold. Chill until firm. Unmold on a bed of lettuce and garnish with the black olives.

*Serves 8 to 10.*

## SHRIMP AND RICE a la SUISSE

1 C long grain rice
3 T butter, melted
1 medium onion, chopped
1 green pepper, chopped
1 clove garlic, minced
1-1/2 tsp salt
2-1/2 C hot water
2 lbs raw shrimp, peeled and deveined
1/2 lb Swiss cheese, shredded
1/3 C evaporated milk

Brown rice in the melted butter. Add onion, pepper and garlic and cook until onion is golden. Add salt and hot water, place shrimp on top and cover. Cook over low heat 30 to 40 minutes or until the rice is done. Check that water does not cook away. Combine the Swiss cheese and the evaporated milk in a saucepan and cook, stirring constantly, over low heat until the cheese melts and the mixture is hot. Serve the cheese mixture in a separate sauce dish.

*Serves 6 to 8.*

# CURRIED SHRIMP

2-1/2 lbs raw shrimp in shells, or 1-1/2 lbs cleaned
1/2 tsp salt
1/4 tsp pepper
1 onion, sliced
1 lemon, sliced
1/4 C butter
1-1/2 T curry powder
3/4 C onions, chopped
3/4 C apples, peeled and diced
1 beef bouillon cube
1 C hot water
1/2 T cornstarch
3 T cold water
1/2 C light cream

Place shrimp in a large pan with water to cover. Add the salt, pepper, onion slices, and lemon slices. Bring to a boil and cook until the shrimp are pink, about 1 to 2 minutes. Drain and set aside. When cool, remove shrimp shells and devein. Melt butter in a large skillet. Add the curry, chopped onions, and the apples. Sauté this mixture for 10 minutes, stirring constantly. Add the bouillon cube dissolved in the hot water. Simmer, stirring constantly, for 10 minutes. Combine cornstarch with the cold water and add to the mixture in the skillet. Stir until mixture thickens. Add the shrimp and the cream to the skillet mixture. Mix together until thickened, but do not overcook.

*Serves 8.*

# Chapter 6
# CHAFING DISH
# SPECIALTIES

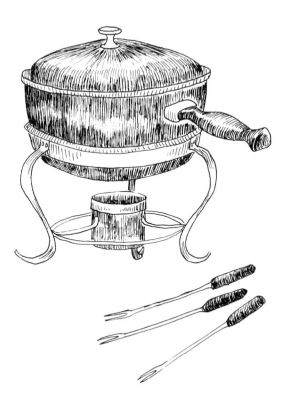

# RUMAKI

2 T butter
1 lb chicken livers
1 can (7 oz) water chestnuts
1/2 lb bacon

Melt the butter in a heavy frying pan. Sauté the chicken livers until just golden. Remove and cut into bite-sized pieces. Cut water chestnuts into thirds. Cut bacon slices into thirds. Wrap a piece of bacon around 1 piece of chicken liver and 1 piece of water chestnut. Secure with a toothpick. Broil about 5 inches from the broiler heat for 5 minutes. Turn and continue broiling until bacon is done. Keep warm. Serve with *Rumaki Sauce* (below).

## RUMAKI SAUCE

1 C soy sauce
1 T sugar
1/2 tsp ginger
1/2 tsp garlic powder
1/2 tsp cinnamon

Combine all ingredients. Cook over low heat and stir until the sugar is dissolved. Pour hot sauce in chafing dish. Add the Rumaki and serve.

*Serves 8 to 10.*

## SPANISH RICE au GRATIN

2 T onion, chopped
1-1/2 T green pepper, chopped
1-1/2 T celery, chopped
1-1/2 tsp cooking oil
1 C cooked rice
1 C canned tomatoes
1/2 tsp salt
3/4 tsp sugar
1/8 tsp Worcestershire sauce
1/2 C Romano cheese, grated (another hard cheese may
    be used if desired)

Cook onion, green pepper and celery in the cooking oil until the onion is golden brown. Add the cooked rice, tomatoes, salt, sugar, and Worcestershire sauce. Simmer until mixture thickens, stirring occasionally. Add cheese and stir until it melts. Transfer to a chafing dish and serve.

*Serves 6.*

## MEDITERRANEAN BEEF STEW

4 lbs lean beef, chuck or round steak
1/4 C cooking oil
1 can (6 oz) tomato paste
1-1/2 C red wine
1/4 tsp black pepper
1-1/2 T ground allspice
2 garlic cloves, halved
5 whole cloves
Salt to taste
3 lbs small white onions, peeled

Cut the meat into 1-inch squares and sauté in the cooking oil until brown. Add all other ingredients except the onions and bring to a boil. Cover and simmer for 1 hour. Add onions, more wine if necessary, and simmer another 30 to 40 minutes or until the onions are tender. Discard the garlic and the cloves. Pour into a chafing dish and serve.

*Serves 12.*

## FONDUE

2 lbs Swiss cheese (1 lb Swiss cheese and 1 lb Romano may be substituted)
4 T flour
1/2 tsp garlic salt
1/4 tsp nutmeg
1/2 bottle white wine (reserve the remaining half)
2 T kirsch
2 loaves French or Italian bread, cut into 1-inch cubes with some crust on each piece

Grate the cheese finely, sprinkling it with flour as you grate. Toss with fingers to mix together thoroughly. Add the garlic salt and the nutmeg. Pour wine in the chafing dish, and heat over a very low flame until the wine bubbles. Sprinkle in the cheese mixture slowly, blending with a wooden spoon until all the cheese is melted and the mixture thickens. Add kirsch. Put chafing dish over the alcohol flame and serve with bowls of the cubed bread. May also be set over a pan of hot water if not served immediately.

Add more wine if the mixture begins to thicken.

*Serves 6 to 8.*

# SWEDISH MEATBALLS

2 eggs, slightly beaten
1 C milk
1/2 C dry bread crumbs
3 T butter
1/2 C onion, finely chopped
1-1/2 lbs lean ground chuck
1-3/4 tsp salt
3/4 tsp dill
1/4 tsp allspice
1/8 tsp nutmeg
3 T flour
1/8 tsp pepper
1 beef bouillon cube
1 C boiling water
1/2 C light cream

In a large bowl combine the eggs, milk, and the dry bread crumbs. Melt 1 T butter in large skillet. Sauté the chopped onion until golden, about 5 minutes. Remove onion from the skillet and add to the bread crumb mixture. Add the ground meat, 1-1/2 tsp salt, 1/4 tsp dill, and the allspice and nutmeg, and mix thoroughly. Refrigerate, covered, for 1 hour. Shape into 1-inch meatballs. Add the remaining 2 tablespoons of butter to skillet. Brown meatballs, about one half at a time and when browned, set aside. Add flour to the pan drippings. Stir until smooth. Add remaining 1/4 tsp salt, pepper, and 1/2 teaspoon dill. Dissolve the bouillon cube in the boiling water. Gradually stir the bouillon into mixture in the pan. Heat to the boiling point, stirring constantly. Remove from heat and stir in the cream and the meatballs. Simmer over a low heat for 30 minutes. Transfer to a chafing dish.

*Serves 8 to 10.*

# MEATBALLS IN BURGUNDY SAUCE

1 lb lean ground beef
1/2 C corn flakes, crumbled
1 small onion, minced
3/4 tsp cornstarch
1 egg, beaten
1 T Worcestershire sauce
1/4 C chili sauce
1/2 C evaporated milk
1 tsp salt
1/8 tsp allspice

In a mixing bowl combine the beef, corn flakes, onion, cornstarch, egg, Worcestershire sauce, chili sauce, milk, salt, and allspice and mix well. Shape into 1-inch diameter balls. Place on a cookie sheet with sides or in a large flat roasting pan. Bake at 400°F. for 10 to 15 minutes.

*SAUCE*

2-1/4 T cornstarch
1 C water
2 beef bouillon cubes
3/4 C Burgundy wine
1/2 tsp salt
1/8 tsp pepper

Combine the sauce ingredients in a saucepan. Cook over medium heat, stirring constantly, until sauce thickens and boils. Transfer hot sauce to chafing dish. Add the meatballs and serve.

*Serves 8.*

# SPEEDY SWEET AND SOUR MEATBALLS

1 egg, lightly beaten
1 lb lean ground beef
1 bottle (12 oz) chili sauce
1 jar (8 oz) currant jelly

Mix the egg and the meat. Form into 1-inch balls. Mix the chili sauce and the jelly together in a heavy saucepan, and heat. Drop the meatballs into the sauce and simmer for 30 minutes, stirring occasionally. Add a little water if the sauce gets too dry. Transfer to chafing dish and serve with hot French bread or biscuits.

*Serves 6 to 8.*

# BEEF ROLLMOPS

4 slices round steak, about 1/4 inch thick
1/2 lb bacon
Salt to taste
Fresh ground pepper to taste
2 T butter
1 medium onion, chopped
2 C water
2 T flour
1/2 C water

Cut round steaks into 1-1/2 x 4-inch strips. Cut bacon slices in half crosswise. Lay strip of round steak flat. Cover with a piece of bacon. Sprinkle with salt and pepper to taste. Roll up jellyroll fashion and tie with a string. Melt the butter in a heavy pan. Brown the rollmops on all sides. Add the chopped onions and sauté until the onion is golden. Add the 2 cups of water and heat to boiling. Reduce heat, cover and simmer for 2 hours, or until fork tender. Remove the rollmops and place in a chafing dish.

Combine flour with the 1/2 cup of water. Add to the gravy in the pan. Stir over medium heat until gravy thickens. Correct seasonings. Pour gravy over the rollmops and serve in dish.

*Serves 6 to 8.*


## BRAISED BEEF WITH PEAS AND MUSHROOMS

1-1/2 lbs beef, cut into 1-inch cubes
2 T butter
1/2 tsp salt
1/2 tsp fresh ground black pepper
1/2 C cold water
1 can (10-1/2 oz) mushroom steak sauce
1 can (17 oz) small early peas, drained
2 T butter
6 medium sized fresh mushrooms, sliced
1/2 C sour cream

Brown meat in melted butter in large frying pan. Add salt, pepper and water. Cover and simmer until meat is tender, about 45 minutes. Check while simmering and add more water if necessary. Stir in the sauce and the drained peas. Bring just to a boil. In a small frying pan, melt the butter. Sauté sliced fresh mushrooms. Remove meat and pea mixture from heat and add the sour cream. Transfer to chafing dish and top with the sautéed mushrooms.

*Serves 6.*

# MEATBALL MEDLEY

2 lbs lean ground beef
4 slices white bread, grated into crumbs
5 T grated Romano cheese
1/4 tsp salt
1/4 tsp pepper
1 onion, grated
2 eggs
2 T butter

In a mixing bowl combine the beef, crumbs, cheese, salt, pepper, onion, and eggs. Shape into 1-inch balls and brown in melted butter. While meatballs are browning make the sauce.

*SAUCE*

3 T olive oil
2 onions, chopped
3 green peppers, cut into 1-inch squares
1 can (1 lb) marinara sauce
1 can (1 lb) kidney beans

Heat the olive oil in a large frying pan. Sauté the onions and green peppers until lightly browned, about 5 minutes. Add the marinara sauce and the kidney beans. Heat thoroughly. As the meatballs brown, add to the sauce. Stir occasionally. Simmer for 15 minutes and transfer to a chafing dish.

*Serves 10 to 12.*

# BEEF BALLS IN SOUR CREAM SAUCE

1 egg
3/4 C milk
1/3 C fine dry bread crumbs
1-1/2 tsp salt
1/2 tsp pepper
2 T parsley, minced
1-1/2 lbs lean ground beef
1/4 C butter
3/4 C onions, chopped
3/4 lb fresh mushrooms, sliced
1 tsp paprika
3 T flour
1-1/2 C beef stock
1 tsp Worcestershire sauce
Salt to taste
Pepper to taste
1/2 C sour cream

Beat the egg and milk together. Add the bread crumbs, salt and pepper and mix well. Add the parsley and the meat to the mixture. Mix and form into 1-inch balls. Melt 2 tablespoons of the butter in a large frying pan and brown the meatballs. Remove the meatballs and add the remaining butter to the pan juices. Stir until the butter melts. Add the onions, mushrooms, and the paprika. Sauté until the onions are golden. Add the flour and beef stock and stir until smooth. Add the Worcestershire sauce and the salt and pepper to taste. Blend thoroughly. Return the meatballs to the sauce and cook over low heat for 20 minutes. Stir occasionally. Transfer to the chafing dish. Add sour cream and stir gently. Serve with noodles as a side dish if desired.

*Serves 6 to 8.*

# HERBED MEATBALLS

1 C bread crumbs
1/4 C milk
2 lbs lean ground beef
1 small onion, grated
2 eggs, beaten
1/2 tsp salt
1/4 tsp pepper
1 tsp basil
1 tsp parsley flakes
1 tsp marjoram
3 T butter, melted
1-1/2 C beef consomme
1-1/2 C sour cream
1 T flour

Soak bread crumbs in the milk. Mix with the meat, onion, beaten eggs, salt, pepper, basil, parsley, and the marjoram. Shape into 1-inch balls and brown in the melted butter. Mix consomme, sour cream and flour. Pour over the meatballs. Cover tightly and simmer for 30 minutes. Transfer to a chafing dish.

*Serves 8.*

# SEAFOOD SUPREME

1 pkg (6 oz) frozen Alaskan king crabmeat
1 pkg (10 oz) frozen shrimp in shell
1 pkg (10-1/2 oz) frozen rock lobster tails
1 can (10 oz) frozen shrimp soup
1 can (10 oz) cream of mushroom soup
1 C light cream
3 T white wine
1/4 tsp nutmeg (paprika may be substituted)

Defrost crabmeat. Cook frozen shrimp and lobster tails as directed on packages. Shell lobster tails and shrimp. Check over the crabmeat and be sure it is clean. Cut all seafood into bite-sized pieces. Combine soups, cream and wine in saucepan. Heat just to the boiling point. Add seafood, and transfer to a chafing dish. Top with nutmeg or paprika.

*Serves 8.*

## SEAFOOD CONFETTI

1/2 C green pepper, chopped
1/2 C onion, chopped
1/2 C celery, chopped
1/4 C butter
1/4 C flour
1/2 tsp garlic salt
1/2 tsp salt
1/4 tsp paprika
1/4 tsp pepper
1 can (4 oz) mushroom pieces, undrained
1 pkg (7 oz) frozen shrimp
1 pkg (6 oz) frozen crabmeat, picked over
1 can (5 oz) water chestnuts, drained and sliced
1/3 C sherry
1 C Cheddar cheese, shredded

Sauté the green pepper, onion and the celery in the butter in a large pan until tender, about 10 minutes. Blend in the flour, garlic salt, salt, paprika, and the pepper. Cook until bubbly. Add the mushrooms, shrimp, crabmeat, water chestnuts and the sherry. Stir and simmer, covered, for 20 minutes. Blend in the cheese and stir until melted. Pour into chafing dish and serve with rice or wild rice in side dishes.

*Serves 8 to 10.*

# Chapter 7
# VEGETABLES
# AND PASTA

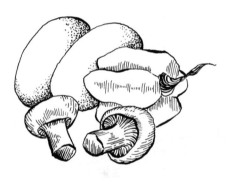

## BAKED BARLEY

1/2 C butter
1 medium onion, chopped
2 C barley
4 C chicken bouillon
1/2 tsp salt
1/2 tsp pepper
1 tsp parsley flakes

Melt butter in a skillet. Sauté onion until golden. Add barley and cook, stirring constantly, until barley is golden. Transfer to a casserole and add remaining ingredients. Mix thoroughly and cover tightly. Bake in a 325°F. oven for 30 minutes or until barley is tender.

*Serves 8 to 10.*


## HONEY GLAZED BEETS

1 can (16 oz) sliced beets, drained
3 T lemon juice
1 tsp lemon rind, grated
1/2 tsp salt
1/2 C honey
2 T butter

Arrange beets in heatproof, shallow serving dish. Sprinkle with lemon juice, rind and salt. Pour honey over all and dot with butter. Cover and bake in 350°F. oven for 15 minutes, or until glaze is slightly browned.

*Serves 4.*

# CANDIED CARROTS

1 dozen medium carrots
Boiling salted water
1/2 C butter
1/2 C brown sugar, firmly packed
1/2 tsp allspice

Scrape carrots and cut into julienne strips. Cook in boiling salted water for 10 minutes, or until tender. Drain well. Melt butter, add sugar and allspice. Stir until well blended. Place carrots in ovenproof dish. Pour butter sauce over carrots and bake in 350°F. oven for 15 minutes.

*Serves 8.*

# BROCCOLI ITALIAN

3 pkgs frozen broccoli spears
2 T olive oil
4 T butter
1 clove garlic
3/4 C grated Parmesan cheese

Partly defrost broccoli. In a large skillet heat the olive oil and butter. Cut garlic in half and sauté until golden. Remove the garlic and spread the broccoli in a single layer in the pan. Sauté, turning gently, for 10 minutes, or until tender. Arrange in a flameproof serving dish. Sprinkle with cheese and place under broiler for about 1 minute.

*Serves 6 to 8.*

## CELERY ORIENTAL

6 stalks celery
1 can (5 oz) water chestnuts
2 T peanut oil
1/4 C slivered almonds
1/2 C beef bouillon
1 T soy sauce

Slice celery in diagonal slices, about 1 inch wide. Slice each water chestnut into thirds. Heat oil in heavy frying pan and sauté celery, water chestnuts and almonds for 3 minutes over high heat, stirring constantly. Reduce heat and add beef bouillon and soy sauce. Simmer, covered, for 2 minutes, or until vegetables are crisp-cooked.

*Serves 6 to 8.*

## GREEN BEANS AMANDINE

3 pkgs (9 oz each) frozen green beans
1/2 C butter
1/2 C sliced, blanched, almonds

Cook green beans according to package directions. Melt butter in separate pan and lightly brown the almonds. Drain beans and transfer to warm serving dish. Pour butter and almonds over beans and toss lightly.

*Serves 8.*

# BAKED CUCUMBERS

4 large cucumbers
2 T onion, chopped
2 T parsley, chopped
4 T butter, melted
1 C bread crumbs
1 C tomatoes, diced
1 tsp salt
1/4 tsp pepper

Pare the cucumbers and cut them in half lengthwise. Scoop out as much of the center pulp portion as possible without breaking the fleshy part. Reserve. Parboil the cucumber shells in lightly salted water for 10 minutes. Drain. Dice the center pulp. Meanwhile, sauté the onion and parsley in the melted butter until the onion is golden. Add the bread crumbs, tomatoes, salt, pepper, and cucumber pulp. Cook 5 minutes longer. Fill the cucumber shells with the hot stuffing and place in a shallow baking dish with a 1/4 inch of water over the bottom. Bake in a 375°F. oven 15 minutes, or until the stuffing has browned on top. Serve in baking dish.

*Serves 8.*

# EGGPLANT PIE

1/4 C green pepper, chopped
1/4 C onion, chopped
1/4 C butter
1 C spaghetti sauce with mushrooms
1/4 tsp salt
3 C eggplant, sliced and quartered
1 9-inch unbaked pastry shell
2 C Mozzarella cheese, shredded

Sauté green pepper and onion in butter in skillet until tender. Blend in spaghetti sauce with mushrooms and salt. Bring to a boil. Add eggplant. Cook loosely covered, stirring occasionally, for 10 minutes, or until eggplant is almost tender. Place half of eggplant mixture in pie shell. Top with half of the cheese. Add the rest of the eggplant mixture and top with the rest of the cheese. Bake at 400°F. for 30 minutes. Let stand 10 to 15 minutes before cutting into wedges.

*Serves 8.*


## EGGPLANT CAPONATA

1 medium-size eggplant
6 firm, ripe tomatoes
3 medium-size zucchini
2 green peppers
1 sweet red pepper
1/3 C olive oil
2 cloves garlic, minced
1 tsp salt
1/2 tsp seasoned pepper

Wash vegetables. Remove stem from eggplant but leave skin on. Cut into 1-inch cubes. Peel tomatoes and cut into eighths. Remove stems from zucchini and cut into 1/2-inch slices. Seed the green and red peppers and cut into 1-inch squares. Heat olive oil in a large frying pan. Add garlic and sauté for 2 minutes. Add all the other vegetables, salt and seasoned pepper. Continue cooking, stirring gently, until vegetables are lightly browned. Cover pan tightly and continue cooking for about 1 hour, or until vegetables are tender. Stir occasionally. May be served either hot or cold.

*Serves 6 to 8.*

# GREEN BEANS AU GRATIN

2 pkgs (9 oz each) frozen green beans, juilienne cut
2 T butter
1 medium onion, chopped
2 T flour
2 T water
1 tsp salt
1/2 tsp pepper
2 T lemon juice
1 C sour cream
1/2 C Cheddar cheese, shredded
1/2 C dry bread crumbs

Cook green beans following directions on the package. Drain and reserve. Melt butter in frying pan and sauté onion until golden brown. Gradually stir in the flour, water, salt, pepper, and lemon juice. Simmer for 3 minutes. Combine with beans and sour cream. Pour mixture into a greased 2-quart casserole. Top with cheese and bread crumbs. Bake in a 350°F. oven for 30 minutes.

*Serves 8 to 10.*


# STUFFED MUSHROOMS

1 lb medium-size mushrooms
3 T butter
1 tsp onion, grated
1 T parsley, finely chopped
1 clove garlic, minced
3 T white cooking wine
2 T bread crumbs, finely crushed

Wash mushrooms and remove stems. Melt two table-spoons of butter in a heavy frying pan. Chop mushroom stems and sauté in butter with onion, parsley and garlic for 4 minutes. Add wine and cook for 1 minute longer. Add bread crumbs and mix thoroughly. Remove from pan and reserve. Melt remaining 1 T of butter in pan and brown the rounded side of mushroom caps. Place mushroom caps on lightly greased broiler pan. Fill with chopped mushroom stem mixture, and put under broiler for about 5 minutes, or until brown.

*Serves 8.*

## MUSHROOM QUICHE

2 T butter
1/4 lb fresh mushrooms, sliced
1 9-inch unbaked pie shell
4 eggs
1 T flour
Dash nutmeg
2 C half-and-half cream
2 C Swiss cheese, grated

Melt butter in frying pan and sauté mushroom slices until golden brown. Place mushrooms in pie shell. In a mixing bowl, beat together the eggs, flour, nutmeg, and cream. Pour over mushrooms. Sprinkle Swiss cheese evenly over pie. Bake in 375°F. oven for approximately 40 minutes. The quiche is done when a knife inserted near the center comes away clean.

*Serves 6 to 8.*

# SCALLOPED POTATOES WITH CREAM

3 T parsley, finely chopped
1/2 tsp marjoram
1/2 tsp thyme
1/2 tsp sage
1/2 tsp salt
1/4 tsp pepper
6 medium potatoes, peeled and sliced
1 medium onion, finely chopped
1-1/2 C heavy cream

Mix together all the seasonings. In lightly greased casserole put a layer of potatoes. Sprinkle with mixed seasonings and chopped onion. Repeat layers until all ingredients have been used. Pour on heavy cream and cover tightly with aluminum foil. Bake in a 400°F. oven for 30 minutes. Remove foil and bake an additional 30 minutes, until top is browned and potatoes are tender.

*Serves 6 to 8.*

# POTATOES GRUYERE

6 medium potatoes
1-1/2 tsp salt
1/2 tsp pepper
3 eggs, beaten
1-1/2 C milk, scalded
1-1/2 C Gruyere cheese, grated
Paprika

Peel potatoes and slice thin. Place in mixing bowl and add salt, pepper, beaten eggs, scalded milk and half the cheese. Mix well. Pour into a large, well greased, shallow baking dish and sprinkle the remaining cheese on top.

Dust lightly with paprika. Bake in 350°F. oven for one hour or until potatoes are done and top is brown.

*Serves 8.*

## POTATO TOMATO CASSEROLE

4 C potatoes, peeled and thinly sliced
1/2 tsp salt
1/4 tsp pepper
2 ripe tomatoes, diced
1/3 C olive oil
1 garlic clove, minced
3 T parsley, minced
3 T lemon juice

In a greased casserole, arrange sliced potatoes in layers, each seasoned with salt and pepper. Mix the tomatoes, olive oil, garlic, parsley, and lemon juice. Cover the potatoes with tomato mixture and bake in a 350°F. oven for 45 minutes, or until potatoes are done and top is lightly browned.

*Serves 6 to 8.*

# NORMANDY POTATOES

6 medium potatoes
1-1/2 C boiling water
1 envelope onion soup mix
1/4 C butter

Peel the potatoes and slice thin. Arrange in large, well greased, shallow baking dish. Combine boiling water, onion soup mix, and butter. Stir until butter melts. Pour over potatoes. Bake in a 400°F. oven for one hour, or until potatoes are done and liquid is absorbed.

*Serves 8 to 10.*

# STUFFED GREEN PEPPERS

8 green peppers, medium size
4 T butter
1/2 C celery, chopped
2 C cooked rice
1/2 C chili sauce
1 C Swiss cheese, grated
1/2 tsp salt
1/2 C bread crumbs
4 T melted butter

Cut out stem ends of peppers and remove seeds. Parboil peppers 5 minutes in salted water. Drain. Melt butter in pan and cook celery until tender. Add cooked rice, chili sauce, cheese, and salt. Fill peppers with rice mixture, top with bread crumbs and melted butter. Stand peppers in baking dish containing 1/2 inch hot water. Bake at 350°F. until peppers are done and crumbs are browned, about 30 minutes.

*Serves 8.*

## SWEET POTATO AND APPLE CASSEROLE

3 sweet potatoes, medium sized
4 apples, medium sized, pared and cored
1/2 C brown sugar
1/2 tsp salt
3 T butter
1/4 tsp allspice
1/4 C water

Cook the sweet potatoes in boiling water until tender. Cool and peel. Cut the sweet potatoes and apples into slices, and place in alternate layers in a greased baking dish. Sprinkle each layer with sugar and salt, dot top with butter, dust with allspice, add water and cover. Bake in a 350°F. oven for 30 minutes. Uncover, and bake for an additional 15 minutes.

*Serves 6 to 8.*


## CREAMED SPINACH

2 pkgs frozen spinach, chopped
1/3 C sour cream
1/2 tsp nutmeg

Cook spinach following directions on package. Drain well. Stir in sour cream and transfer to a heated serving dish. Dust with nutmeg.

*Serves 8 to 10.*

## BROILED TOMATOES

4 large, firm tomatoes
4 T butter
1 tsp oregano
Salt to taste
Pepper to taste
1/2 C grated Parmesan cheese

Cut tomatoes in half and place on aluminum foil in broiler pan. Dot with butter, season with oregano, salt and pepper. Sprinkle with Parmesan cheese and broil lightly about 5 minutes or until cheese melts.

*Serves 8.*


## CHILLED VEGETABLES RIVIERA

1 jar (12 oz) white asparagus tips
2 jars (4 oz each) marinated artichoke hearts
2 jars (5-1/2 oz each) marinated mushrooms
5 T Italian salad dressing

Drain all vegetables, reserving 3 T of artichoke marinade. Arrange asparagus tips on serving platter in wheel spoke fashion, tips pointing out. Pile artichokes in the center. Arrange mushrooms between the spokes. Sprinkle lightly with the 3 T artichoke marinade, cover with plastic wrap and refrigerate. Drizzle salad dressing over vegetables just before serving.

*Serves 6.*

## VEGETABLE CASSEROLE AMANDINE

2 pkgs (10 oz each) mixed vegetables frozen in butter
    sauce, in boiling bag
1-1/2 C uncooked egg noodles
1/4 C onion, chopped
1/4 C celery, chopped
1 can (8 oz) tomato sauce
1/2 C sour cream
1/4 C slivered almonds

Cook vegetables in boiling water as directed on package. Cook noodles in boiling salted water as directed on package to medium firm. Drain noodles. Partially open boiling bags of vegetables and drain butter sauce into small frying pan. Sauté onion and celery in the butter sauce until tender. Combine cooked noodles and mixed vegetables with onion-celery mixture. Add tomato sauce and sour cream. Pour into a 1-1/2 quart casserole and top with almonds. Bake in 350°F. oven for 30 minutes.

*Serves 10 to 12.*

## BOHEMIAN SAUERKRAUT

1 can (29 oz) sauerkraut
1 C beer
1/4 tsp caraway seeds

Drain sauerkraut, rinse in cold water and drain again. In 1-1/2 quart casserole combine the sauerkraut, beer and caraway seeds. Cover and bake in 375°F. oven for 30 minutes.

*Serves 8.*

# FETTUCINI

1 pkg (8 oz) fettucini or egg noodles
1 pkg (8 oz) cream cheese
1/2 lb butter
1/2 C noodle cooking water
1/2 tsp salt
1/4 tsp pepper
1/2 T sugar
1/2 C Parmesan or Romano cheese, grated

Cook fettucini or egg noodles according to directions on package. While noodles are cooking melt the cream cheese and butter over a low flame. Drain noodles and add 1/2 C of the hot water to the cream cheese mixture. Add salt, pepper and sugar to the sauce. Toss the noodles and sauce together in serving dish. Top with grated cheese.

*Serves 6.*

# LONDONDERRY CASSEROLE

8 oz macaroni
2 C milk
2 eggs, well beaten
4 T butter
2 C English Cheddar cheese, shredded
2 C soft bread crumbs
2 T parsley, minced
2 T onion, minced
2 tsp salt
1/2 tsp pepper

Cook macaroni following directions on package. Drain. Heat milk, but do not boil. In a large mixing bowl combine eggs, milk, butter, cheese, bread crumbs, parsley, onion, salt, and pepper. Add macaroni and mix thoroughly. Pour into well greased large casserole, stand in pan containing 1 inch of water, and bake in 350°F. oven for 30 minutes.

*Serves 8 to 10.*

# Chapter 8
# DESSERTS

## MOM'S CHEESE CAKE

1 lb cream cheese
1 lb cottage cheese
1 C sugar
6 eggs, separated
2 T cornstarch
1 tsp vanilla

Rice cream cheese and cottage cheese together in a large mixing bowl. Add sugar, beaten egg yolks, cornstarch and vanilla. Mix well. Beat egg whites until stiff, but not dry, and fold into cheese mixture. Bake in ungreased 9-inch spring pan in preheated 450°F. oven for 5 minutes. Reduce heat to 350°F. and bake for one hour longer. Allow to cool in the oven.

*Serves 12 to 14.*

## PUMPKIN CAKE

1 pkg (18 oz) spice cake mix
1 can (16 oz) pumpkin
1/2 tsp cinnamon
1/4 tsp nutmeg
1/4 tsp cloves
1/4 tsp ginger
1/2 C water
1/2 C brown sugar
3 eggs

Place all ingredients in a large bowl and beat with electric mixer for 5 minutes, until smooth and blended. Grease and flour a 9-inch tube pan. Pour batter into pan and bake in 350°F. oven for 1 hour, or until cake tests done.

*Serves 10 to 14.*

# GRANDMA'S GRAHAM CRACKER CAKE

1/2 C shortening
1 C sugar
3 eggs, separated
1 C milk
2 dozen graham crackers (2 C crumbs)
2 tsp baking powder
1/2 tsp salt
1 C chopped nuts
1 C heavy cream
1/4 C confectioners' sugar

Cream shortening and sugar together. Add egg yolks and beat well. Add milk. Roll crackers into fine crumbs and add to egg mixture. Add baking powder, salt and nuts. Stir thoroughly. Beat egg whites until stiff and fold into batter. Pour into 2 greased and floured 9-inch layer cake pans. Bake in 375°F oven for 20 to 25 minutes, or until cake tests done. When cool, whip cream with sugar. Spread sweetened whipped cream between the layers and on the top.

*Serves 8 to 10.*

# GEORGIA PEACH CAKE

6 eggs
1 C sugar
1/8 tsp salt
1/2 tsp vanilla
1 C sifted cake flour
1/4 C melted butter
1 C heavy cream
1/4 C confectioners' sugar
2 C peach slices

In a large mixing bowl beat the eggs with an electric mixer until thick and lemon colored. Gradually add the sugar. Beat until fluffy. Add the salt and vanilla. Fold in the sifted cake flour. Fold in the melted butter. Pour into 2 greased and floured 9-inch layer cake pans. Bake in a 350°F. oven 25 minutes, or until cake tests done. Immediately remove from cake pans and cool on cake racks. When cool split layers with a sharp knife. Whip the cream and add the confectioners' sugar. Combine with the peach slices and spread on the layers of the cake. Place the completed cake on a serving plate and cut into 8 or 10 wedges. Cover, and refrigerate for at least 2 hours.

*Serves 8 to 10.*

## JEAN'S APPLESAUCE CAKE

1/2 C butter
1 C sugar
1 egg
1 tsp vanilla
1 jar (15 oz) applesauce
2 C flour, sifted
2 tsp baking soda
1/2 tsp cinnamon
1/4 tsp cloves
1 C golden raisins
1 C chopped nuts

Cream the butter and sugar. Add egg, vanilla and applesauce. Sift flour with other dry ingredients and add to applesauce mixture. Blend well. Stir in the raisins and nuts. Pour into a greased and floured 9 x 5-inch loaf pan and bake in a 350°F. oven for 1 hour, or longer, until loaf tests done.

*Serves 8 to 10.*

## LAURENTIAN RUM CAKE

3/4 C butter
1-1/2 C light brown sugar, firmly packed
1 C pitted dates, chopped
1 C walnuts, chopped
1 tsp baking soda
1 C boiling water
3 eggs
2-1/4 C flour, sifted
3/4 tsp salt
3 T dark rum

Cream butter and sugar until light. Add dates and nuts. Mix baking soda with boiling water and combine with the date and nut mixture. Beat eggs until well beaten. Add eggs, flour and salt to butter mixture. Beat until smooth. Add rum and blend well. Pour into greased pan (13 x 9 x 2) and bake in slow oven (300°F.) for 1-1/4 hours, or until cake tests done. Cool in pan on rack for 10 minutes and then remove. This cake may be served plain or frosted with confectioners' sugar glaze and topped with additional halved walnuts.

*Serves 10 to 12.*


## CHOCOLATE SPICE UPSIDE-DOWN CAKE

1 C semisweet chocolate morsels
2/3 C sweetened condensed milk
2 T water
1 tsp vanilla
1 pkg (18 oz) spice cake mix
1/2 C walnuts, large pieces

Melt semisweet chocolate morsels over hot (not boiling) water. Remove from heat and add condensed milk, water and vanilla. Stir until smooth. Line bottom and sides of 12 x 8 x 2-inch baking dish with double thickness of heavy aluminum foil. Pour in chocolate mixture. Prepare cake mix according to package directions. Pour gently over chocolate in baking pan. Bake according to package directions until cake tests done. Invert cake on rack. Lift off baking dish. Let stand 2 minutes. Peel off foil. Sprinkle nuts on top. When cool, cut into 15 squares.

*Serves 15.*

## PAULINE'S FRUIT BREAD

1 C sifted flour
1 tsp baking soda
2/3 C sugar
6 eggs, separated
3/4 C raisins
1/2 C chopped dried fruit
3 cardamom seeds, crushed
3/4 C chopped walnuts
1 pkg (6 oz) semisweet chocolate bits

Sift the flour, baking soda and sugar together. Whip egg whites stiff and set aside. Beat egg yolks and combine with the flour mixture. Add remaining ingredients to the flour mixture. Fold in egg whites. Pour into greased and floured 9 x 5-inch loaf pan. Bake in 300°F. oven for 1 hour, or until loaf tests done. Let stand until thoroughly cool before slicing. Slice thin with sharp knife.

*Serves 10 to 12.*

# GOLD STAR CARROT CAKE

1 C sugar
1/2 C salad oil
1-1/2 C flour, sifted
2 tsp baking powder
1 tsp baking soda
1/4 tsp salt
3/4 tsp cinnamon
1 C carrots, grated
2 eggs
1/2 C walnuts, chopped
Confectioners' sugar for glazing
6 walnut halves

Mix sugar and oil. Sift dry ingredients together and add to sugar mixture. Add carrots and blend well. Beat eggs and add to carrot mixture. Add chopped nuts and mix thoroughly. Pour into greased and floured star-shaped pan. (A 9 x 5-inch loaf pan may be used if desired.) Cover with aluminum foil. Bake in a 350°F. oven for 20 minutes. Remove the foil and continue baking 40 minutes longer, or until cake tests done. Ice with confectioners' sugar glaze and decorate with walnut halves.

*Serves 10 to 12.*

# LINZER TORTE

1 C butter
1 C sugar
2 egg yolks
1 hard-cooked egg yolk, sieved
1 lemon, juiced, the rind grated
1 tsp vanilla
1/2 lb almonds, ground
2 C sifted flour
1 tsp baking powder
1 C raspberry jam
Confectioners' sugar

Cream butter and gradually beat in the sugar. Add raw egg yolks, sieved hard-cooked egg yolk, lemon juice and rind, and the vanilla. Stir in the almonds, flour and baking powder. With your fingers, work into a smooth dough. Divide dough in half. Press half into the bottom and sides of a fully greased removable bottom 9-inch cake pan, making bottom layer thicker than the sides. Cover with 3/4 cup of jam. Chill remaining half of dough for 15 minutes. Roll thin and cut into 3/8-inch strips. Criss-cross over top. Bake in 350°F. oven for 45 to 50 minutes, or until pale gold. Remove from oven and immediately fill spaces between strips with remaining jam. Dust with confectioners' sugar.

*Serves 10.*

# CREAM PUFFS

1 C water
1/2 C butter
1/4 tsp salt
1 C sifted flour
4 large eggs

Place the water, butter, and salt in a 2-quart saucepan. Bring to boiling point. Remove from heat and stir in all the flour at one time, using a wooden spoon. Return to heat and cook, stirring vigorously, until mixture leaves sides of pan and forms a compact ball. Remove from heat and cool slightly. Add eggs, one at a time, beating well after each addition until mixture is smooth and glossy. Drop by tablespoonful about 2 inches apart onto unoiled cookie sheet. Bake in preheated 400°F. oven for 45 minutes, until puffs are light and dry. Turn off heat. Prick puffs with knife to allow steam to escape and let them cool in the oven for 20 minutes. Remove from oven, cut open, and fill puffs with custard, sweetened whipped cream, or ice cream. Dust with confectioners' sugar.

*Makes 12 puffs.*

# RUM CHERRY ELEGANTE

1 C rice
4 C milk
1 T (1 envelope) unflavored gelatin
1/4 C rum
2 egg yolks
1 tsp vanilla extract
1-1/4 C sugar
3/4 C glacéed cherries
2 T water

Combine rice and milk in top of double boiler. Cook over boiling water, stirring occasionally, for 45 minutes. Meanwhile, soften gelatin in rum. Add to rice with egg yolks, vanilla, and 3/4 cup of the sugar. Mix well. Stir in cherries. Melt remaining sugar with 2 T water in a small pan. Stir constantly until it carmelizes. Remove immediately from heat and pour into pudding mold. Dip mold into cold water to chill. Tip mold in all directions so that it is completely lined with caramel. When it stops running set to cool. When rice mixture has cooled pour it into the mold and refrigerate until set. Unmold and serve.

*Serves 10 to 12.*


## IRENE'S MOUSSE


1/2 pt heavy cream
1/4 C sugar
1/4 C milk
1 tsp vanilla

Whip the cream until it starts to thicken. Add sugar. Continue beating and very gradually add the milk. Stir in the vanilla and pour into freezing tray. Freeze for at least 3 hours. Serve in sherbert glass.

*Serves 6.*

# DOT'S STRAWBERRY BAVARIAN

1 pkg frozen strawberries
Cold water
1 pkg strawberry-flavored gelatin
1 C boiling water
1 C heavy cream

Defrost strawberries and drain. Measure strawberry juice and add enough cold water to make one cup. Combine gelatin with hot water and stir until gelatin dissolves. Add strawberry juice and refrigerate until thickened. Whip until doubled in bulk. Stir in the strawberries. Whip the cream and fold into the strawberry mixture. Pour into serving dish. Cover with plastic wrap and return to refrigerator. Chill until firm.

*Serves 8.*

# BLACK CHERRY MONTE CARLO

1 can (2 lb) pitted black cherries
2 T butter
1-1/2 T cornstarch
2 T sugar
2 T cherry liqueur
8 slices plain pound cake

Drain cherries. In saucepan, melt butter, add juice from cherries, mix well. Add cornstarch and sugar, stir until smooth. Heat, stirring constantly, until clear and thickened. Remove from heat. Add cherries and cherry liqueur. Put cake on individual plates and pour cherry sauce over the slices.

*Serves 8.*

# MOCHA SPANISH CREAM

1 envelope (1 T) unflavored gelatin
6 T sugar
2 T instant coffee
2 T cocoa
2 eggs, separated
2 C milk
1 tsp vanilla extract
1 T Kahlua or other coffee-flavored liqueur
3 T sliced almonds

Combine gelatin, 2 tablespoons of the sugar, instant coffee and cocoa in saucepan. Beat together egg yolks and milk. Pour into gelatin mixture and stir until blended. Place over low heat and stir constantly until gelatin dissolves and mixture thickens slightly, about 3 to 5 minutes. Remove from heat and stir in vanilla extract and Kahlua. Cool in refrigerator stirring occasionally, until mixture mounds slightly when dropped from the spoon. Beat egg whites until stiff but not dry. Gradually add remaining 4 T sugar, and beat until very stiff. Fold in gelatin mixture. Pour into 4-cup mold. Chill until firm. Unmold and garnish with sliced almonds.

*Serves 6 to 8.*

## ROSE WINE GELATIN

2 envelopes (1 T each) unflavored gelatin
1 C cold water
1 C sugar
2 C Rosé wine
3 T lemon juice
1 C heavy cream, whipped

Sprinkle gelatin over water in saucepan. Let stand for 5 minutes until gelatin softens. Place over low heat and stir constantly until gelatin dissolves. Add sugar and continue stirring until sugar dissolves. Remove from heat. Stir in wine and lemon juice. Pour into 4 cup heart-shaped mold. Chill until firm. Unmold and garnish with whipped cream.

*Serves 6 to 8.*

## CANTALOUPE KIRSCH

1 large cantaloupe
1 pint fresh strawberries
1 pint fresh blueberries
1/4 lb seedless green grapes
2 T sugar
1/2 C Kirsch

Seed cantaloupe and cut into balls. Wash and hull strawberries. Wash and remove stems from blueberries. Wash grapes. Combine all fruit with sugar and Kirsch in a bowl and mix thoroughly. Cover and refrigerate at least 2 hours. Stir occasionally.

*Serves 8 to 10.*

## DONNA'S HOT FUDGE DELIGHT

2 (3 oz) chocolate bars with almonds
2 T cream
1 T orange-flavored liqueur (or rum)
6 slices plain pound cake
6 large scoops ice cream
3 T slivered almonds

Melt chocolate bars in top of double boiler. When melted blend in cream and the liqueur. Keep warm over hot water. Toast cake. Put cake on individual serving plates. Put ice cream on top of cake slices. Pour hot fudge sauce over all and top with slivered almonds.

*Serves 6.*

## PINEAPPLE ISLAND DELIGHT

1 can (1 lb, 14 oz) pineapple slices
1/4 C butter
1 C apricot-pineapple preserves
1/2 C rum
8 scoops vanilla or pineapple ice cream (about 1 qt)
2 T crystalized ginger, minced

Drain pineapple and reserve 6 tablespoons of the syrup. Melt butter in large frying pan, add pineapple slices and sauté until lightly browned. Stir in reserved pineapple syrup and apricot-pineapple preserves. Heat and stir gently until pineapple looks glazed. Warm rum in small pan over low heat. Pour rum over pineapple slices in pan and ignite. Put ice cream scoops in individual serving dishes. When flames die down stir sauce gently. Arrange pineapple slices around ice cream. Pour hot sauce over all, and garnish with ginger.

*Serves 8.*

## CHERRIES JUBILEE

1 can (1 lb, 4 oz) pitted Bing cherries
1 T cornstarch
1 T cold water
1 qt vanilla ice cream
1/2 C cherry-flavored brandy

Drain juice from cherries and reserve 1/2 cup. In a saucepan stir cornstarch and water until cornstarch is dissolved. Add cherry juice and cook over low heat, stirring constantly, until sauce thickens slightly. Add cherries and warm through. Transfer cherry sauce to serving dish or a chafing dish. Spoon ice cream into individual dessert dishes. Warm brandy slightly and pour over the cherry sauce. Ignite and ladle over ice cream while still flaming.

*Serves 6 to 8.*


## FESTIVE FRUIT DESSERT

1 pkg (8 oz) cream cheese
1/4 C Marsala wine
1/2 C heavy cream, whipped
1 pkg (4 oz) candied mixed fruit
Assorted fresh fruit (apple slices, pineapple slices, pear
    wedges, melon wedges or balls, orange segments)

Soften cream cheese and beat in Marsala wine. Fold in whipped cream and candied fruit. Arrange fresh fruit attractively on large platter and serve with fruit dip. May be eaten with the fingers.

*Serves 8 to 10.*

# MELON TROPICANA

1 large watermelon
1 cantaloupe
1 honeydew melon
1/4 lb seedless green grapes
4 T honey
2 T lemon juice
1/2 C rum
1 pint fresh ripe strawberries

Cut watermelon in half lengthwise. Scoop out the pulp in shape of small balls with a melon ball cutter. Remove seeds. Scoop cantaloupe and honeydew pulp into balls and combine with watermelon balls in large bowl. Wash and dry grapes and add to melon ball mixture. In separate container combine honey, lemon juice and rum. Pour over fruit mixture, stir, and refrigerate for at least three hours. Stir occasionally. Wash and hull strawberries. Just before serving pile the fruit mixture into the watermelon shell. Garnish edge of watermelon shell with strawberries.

*Serves 12 to 16.*

# Chapter 9
# BEVERAGES

# IRISH COFFEE

1 tsp sugar
1 jigger Irish whisky
1 C hot black coffee
Heavy cream, slightly whipped

Combine sugar, Irish whisky and coffee in a stemmed glass. Float whipped cream on top. (There are special Irish Coffee glasses available in the larger stores.)

*Serves 1.*

# GREEK COFFEE

3/4 C Greek coffee*
4-1/2 C cold water
3 T sugar (or less if desired)

Combine all ingredients in a small saucepan. Bring to a boil, allowing mixture to foam. Remove from heat until mixture stops boiling. Return to heat and bring to a full boil a second time. Repeat the last two steps. Pour some of the foam into each demitasse cup. Fill with the remaining coffee.

*Makes 12 demitasse servings.*

* Greek coffee is similar to Turkish coffee. It is a finely pulverized grind available in coffee shops and Greek food stores.

## VIENNESE COFFEE

12 C coffee, extra strong
1/2 pt heavy cream
1 tsp vanilla

    Make the coffee extra strong. Whip the cream, adding the vanilla. Place in a serving bowl. Pour coffee into cups. Serve with sugar and the whipped cream to be spooned on the top.

*Serves 12.*

## CAFE ITALIA

1 C coffee
1 T rum
Twist of lemon
Sugar to taste

    Make coffee using an Italian roast coffee. Pour each serving into a stemmed glass. Add rum and lemon twist to each glass. Serve with sugar.

*Serves 1.*

## SPICED ICE COFFEE

6 C strong hot coffee
4 T sugar
2 cinnamon sticks
10 whole cloves
10 whole allspice
2 peppercorns

158

Combine all ingredients in a large container. Let steep for at least 1 hour. Strain over cracked ice into tall glasses. Serve with cream and sugar.

*Serves 6 to 8.*

# CAFE MARLENE

1 C instant cocoa mix
1/3 C instant coffee
4 C boiling water
Cream

Combine cocoa mix and coffee. Add the boiling water, stirring constantly. Serve with cream.

*Makes 6 small cups.*

# CAPPUCCINO

6 T freeze dry coffee
4 C boiling water
1 C whipped cream
Cinnamon

Dissolve the coffee in the boiling water. Whip the cream. Place a spoonful of whipped cream in each demitasse cup. Pour hot coffee over the cream. Add a dash of cinnamon to each cup. Serve with sugar.

*Makes 10 demitasse servings.*

## APPLE TEA

Select a firm ripe apple with no blemishes. Place in a small airtight container. Surround with tea bags (about 6 to 8 tea bags to 1 apple). Cover and let stand at room temperature for about 1 week before using. Brew tea in usual way.

## FLOWER TEAS

Deliciously different, fragrant teas, similar to the Chinese Jasmine Tea, may be made at home. Use flowers such as roses, gardenias, carnations, or scented violets. Separate the flower petals and nip off any bitter green edges, which are sometimes found at the base of the petals. Lay the petals flat in a single layer on a paper towel. Keep in a cool dry dark place until thoroughly dry. Mix with tea leaves in an airtight cannister. Let stand several days before using. Exact proportions vary because of flowers used and individual preferences. It is suggested to start with a 7 to 1 ratio of tea to petals. Brew tea in usual way.

## VANILLA TEA

Make as above, substituting a vanilla bean for the dried flower petals.

## CHAMPAGNE FRUIT PUNCH

1 bottle champagne
1/2 C apricot brandy
1 orange, peeled and sliced thin
1/2 C crushed pineapple
1/2 C sliced strawberries
2 T powdered sugar

Combine all ingredients in punch bowl with a block of ice, or a block of frozen orange juice.

*Makes about 20 servings.*

## PARTY PUNCH

1 qt strong tea
1 qt rye whisky
1 pt dark rum
1 pt orange juice
1 C lemon juice
1 qt apple juice

Combine all ingredients in a punch bowl with a block of ice. Freeze fresh fruit such as pineapple slices, orange slices, and cherries in the freezing tray for an attractive ice block.

*Makes about 25 punch cups.*

# KENTUCKY EGGNOG

2 dozen eggs, separated
2-1/2 C bourbon
1 qt heavy cream
6 T sugar
1 C (additional) sugar
Nutmeg to taste

In a large mixing bowl of electric mixer beat egg yolks for 20 minutes, until they are light and very fluffy. Continue beating and add bourbon *very* slowly. This may be done the night before and kept in the refrigerator in a covered container. Just before serving whip the cream until it stands in peaks, then add the 6 tablespoons sugar. Lightly fold in egg yolk mixture. Whip egg whites until they are dry and stand in peaks. Add the 1 cup sugar, one tablespoon at a time, and continue beating for 10 minutes after last spoonful of sugar has been added. Fold egg whites into the egg yolk mixture and blend until well mixed and smooth. Top each cup with a dash of nutmeg.

*Makes 30 servings.*

# INDEX

165

167

172

174

175